The Middle Path
of Life

*Talks on the Practice
of Insight Meditation*

DHIRAVAMSA

Blue Dolphin Publishing

Also by Dhiravamsa

*

THE REAL WAY TO AWAKENING

*

A NEW APPROACH TO BUDDHISM

*

THE DYNAMIC WAY OF MEDITATION

*

THE WAY OF NON-ATTACHMENT

*

TURNING TO THE SOURCE

ISBN 0-931891-22-8

Library of Congress Cataloging-in-Publication Data

Dhiravamsa.
 The middle path of life: talks on the practice of insight meditation/
by Dhiravamsa.
  p.   cm.
 ISBN 0-931892-22-8: $9.95
  1. Meditation—Buddhism.   2. Vipaśyanā (Buddhism)   I. Title.
BQ5620.D48 1988
294.3'443—dc19   88-38455
                                                               CIP

For information, contact
Blue Dolphin Publishing, Inc.
P.O. Box 1908
Nevada City, CA 95959

Printed in the United States of America by
Blue Dolphin Press, Inc.
Grass Valley, California

Cover photo: Miles A. Vich

CONTENTS

DEDICATION

to my boys:
Adam, Jacob, and Orca

PREFACE

DISORDER AND CHAOS have always existed in the world, but perhaps because of the progress in material and scientific attainment, these are much accentuated today. The young generation in particular is aware that this progress has not made people more contented inwardly or made the world a happier place to live in. They search for an alternative to the society we now have.

Disorder and chaos in the world are a reflection of the disorder and chaos in each one of us, and for order to be achieved, it is necessary for each individual to look inwardly and work on himself/herself thoroughly. Without first searching within it is impossible to radically change society. To work on oneself does not mean to be selfish or to be aloof from society; it means to abolish confusion and bring about clarity of mind. Until this is achieved within the individual, it will not be possible to bring about a creative new order in the world.

To help achieve this aim, these talks were given and are reproduced in this book. The author's grateful thanks are due to those friends who have undertaken the arduous task of transcribing the talks, and of checking the English language.

Love and Peace to all beings,
DHIRAVAMSA

September 1973

I

THE MIDDLE PATH OF LIFE

THE MIDDLE PATH of life is a large subject to consider, because it is not easy to define it or to assert a principle or formula for it. Usually we look for something very definite, or for something which is clearly said or named, so that we can follow. You may be disappointed to find that this middle path of life has no clear definition, and in a way it can have no definition at all.

You may remember that the Buddha, soon after enlightenment, was thinking of giving his first sermon to people who could understand his teaching. Firstly he thought of the two teachers under whom he had studied and practised, fulfilling all the spiritual attainments, but whom he had left, realising that he had still not reached enlightenment. He thought they would understand what he was going to say, but then in his insight he saw that they had already died. Then he saw in his mind the five ascetics with whom he had practised self-mortification, and whom he had left because he realised that their extreme asceticism was not the way. He felt they would understand, so he went and gave the sermon to them at Benares.

In his first sermon, the Buddha mentioned the two extreme practices. The first is self-mortification, believing that by tormenting the body, fasting, lying on thorns or nails, depriving and wearing out the physical form, one will realise Nirvana. The other extreme is self-indulgence and hedonism, believing that happiness is the primary goal of life (this can often be seen in modern spiritual movements which aim for states of bliss).

The Buddha taught the middle path which lies beyond these two extremes. This is the Buddhist way of life, which is called the Eightfold Path : right understanding, right thought, right action, right speech, right livelihood, right effort, right awareness, right contemplation. These practices are the foundation of the Buddha's teaching.

We can see that the two extremes are prevalent in our present world. Many people advocate the material way of life, thinking that through material support all happiness must come — but it is not so. We get more and more comfort and pleasure, but we are still not happy because we are not free. Our problems may increase, because when sense desires are continually gratified and the body is richly fed, the mind becomes poorer and more disturbed — it has more thirst, more craving and clinging. With an unstable mind, we go to extremes. When there is no balance in the mind, then there is no balance in life, and this we can see clearly.

The other extreme concerns a 'spiritual' life, in which people may drop away from the material world, refusing to face what is arising in their lives. They may give up their work and responsibilities, renouncing the world without insight into what it is that really needs to be renounced. In fact the world cannot be renounced, because the world means human relationships and life situations which reappear in different forms. If we turn our face away from these, it is the ego rejecting the natural path provided. Even those who go into the forest or become *sannyasis* need to accept material things to support their life, and monks living in a monastery exist within a community. Those who insist on rarefied conditions and resist what is being given to them by life are usually being driven by spiritual ambition. They may become famous teachers, but will still be bound by their own self-importance and desire for power. Their work may appear more profound and valuable than the materialist, but in fact they are developing an equally superficial side of life, limited by what might be called spiritual materialism.

It is not very easy to practise the middle path of life, but that does not mean that it is difficult for us to begin. We have to see the extremes we are practising in life, and to watch ourselves, attending to all our activities. The middle path is the way of balance, neither to the left nor the right, neither to the wrong nor the correct, but we shall not have this balance through trying to grasp it. It will come when the extremes are properly looked at and dissolved. The mind is always wanting to grasp something in order to stay with it and not let it go, but in doing that it is not open, and for the middle path it needs to be open. As soon as we are closed to any event, any situation, we fall asleep psychologically. In sleep we feel comfortable and secure, but there is no freedom. You might say that of course there is freedom, because you can do what you think is right, but that is like the freedom of prisoners to decorate their prisons — they are still living in prison. It is essential to look at the mind and how it creates things to reassure itself.

The middle path is not just the path between two poles, but is beyond them. In the ultimate sense we can say that the middle path of life has no concept of what is right or what is wrong, what is good or what is bad. When we have concepts we try to justify our behaviour by them. Our concepts impose upon us so that we don't really look into the action in order to see it as it is. Usually things are judged according to a standard or an authority, whether religious, political, social, legal, parental or personal, which is secondhand. But if we look for ourselves, without denying all authorities but understanding things at first-hand, we shall have the basis for a balanced way of life.

Guidance is important, but is something we can find within us which fully relates us to the teachings of life without being imposed upon us. What is that something? The guide within is 'insight', which arises naturally through the movement of awareness and observation. What does it mean to have insight? It does not mean that you have seen something very mysterious, beyond the reach of human intelligence. It is something well within the capacity of human beings, although not necessarily expressed in words or concepts. It is the guiding principle in the middle way, but is not a fixed principle and cannot be obtained from studying or any other external source. It is already within every one of us, but its flow is usually blocked by ideas which prevent the seeing within, the *in sight*. To have insight means the clear seeing not only of what lies within us but also outside us, without involving knowledge, but leading to the illumination of knowledge. That kind of seeing has no conclusion, and is therefore free and open to everything.

Let us take the example of insight into pain, which may arise in the body while sitting in meditation. Your first reaction to physical pain may be to try to alter your position in order to be more comfortable. When the pain continues or increases, another kind of pain arises — in the mind, which cannot accept the pain and tries to escape or fight it. If we can *bear* to watch, and keep on watching, we can exercise insight into the situation of pain and of our reactions, which leads to greater insight. Bearing with patience is the key, because when we are watching it does not mean that pain must disappear. We have to allow pain, or even agony, yet without forcing towards a goal of mastery. Let everything happen. If you want to cry, cry, and continue to look. Sometimes the mind and body are suddenly released from pain, and you experience a very pleasant sensation — then look at that too, without interference.

This kind of situation during sitting meditation can give us practice in looking which we can use in life situations. Suppose you are attached to something or somebody, and you lose them. You may feel great loss, and have nothing to cling to. You may feel very lonely, without help from anything external. This is the time to meditate, not in the sense of turning inwards for serenity and security, but in the sense of facing the emptiness and the feelings of loneliness and grief. Look at the situation of loss, and you will have insight into attachment. Go into it fully, with courage. It is the painful way of working, but it is the middle path which eventually dissolves all problems because it turns towards the source — not an imagined source of peace and beauty, but the source of our troubles. When we can look towards the cause of our pain, it ceases to have such power over our lives.

Who can help us to be free unless we are prepared to look? People may give comfort in words and assurances, but this will only be temporary if we do not tread the path ourselves. The problem remains, rooted in the mind, and we have to be willing to experience and investigate it properly, seeing all its aspects. We may sometimes feel despair at the long road ahead, but by being prepared to look fully, just once, our situation changes immediately because we have set our feet in the right direction. Time does not matter, it is the direction that counts. We need not believe what somebody tells us — we need only experiment, and we shall see for ourselves what our path is.

You may ask whether insight gives us any conclusions about what should be done in life. No. 'Should be' and 'Should not be' are ideas. What *is* so is what we deal with, as it arises, and insight will guide our actions. We remain free to act, to lose, to look, to receive, without any rigid decision about what is right or wrong. You may reply that you don't trust your insight at present. But all our actions are based upon something — either our insight or our reactions and desires — so we have to trust the situation which arises. One of our greatest fears is to be ourselves, to accept ourselves as we are. You have to be honest, and not set up high standards, as this can be a form of arrogance. To be yourself is to be alone with what you are, looking at it and at your own reactions to yourself, free from beliefs and objectives. If you say 'It is terrible to be like me. I cannot be like that' you are attempting to escape what is. Reality is not something mysterious and inaccessible — it is what is.

Loneliness can make us feel terrible, because we cannot face ourselves as we are. If we look into the conditioned mind, we shall see why we cannot be alone with it. Can we be alone during our life among people? To be truly alone within life does not mean withdrawal, indifference and pride. It means the allowing of emptiness, through which there is the freedom to open and to listen. If you have the capacity to listen you have the weapon which renders powerless the enemy of authority and compulsion. We cannot listen freely because we still have authority in us, the authority of knowledge, belief, and experience. Sometimes we don't hear other people talking because we are listening to ourselves, interpreting, commenting, rejecting, building up attitudes or evolving questions. With all these you cannot be alone.

The best relationships are based on aloneness, when you do not need to use others for your own happiness or support. Such needs destroy relationships because exploitation is based upon ego wanting, which prevents the giving and accepting of love. If you can lose and be alone, you can share everything with everybody. With such a relationship you will not look back — you can finish with every moment as it passes. Then you do not cling to pleasure. People may think this sounds like a vegetable, without feeling. But at the moment of experience you have pleasure without thought, and that is true pleasure. If desire gives attachment to the experience, and you wish to regain or repeat it, you become out of balance. Leave it alone, so that when you don't regain it, you understand, or when you do, you appreciate it freshly. This is the stage of freedom from experience and non-experience. We don't look back or forward, we don't carry anything with us, so we can travel lightly and freely.

Thinking ahead is often necessary, but when there is attachment to our own wish for success and fear of failure, fear concerning the future creates psychological tension and even paralysis. One cannot act, and it is very difficult to live. But if we can live our life in every moment, appreciating it fully, we can leave it when it is finished.

Life has everything to give, it has all the treasures, but it also has pain because conflict is there. We have to accept life as it is, and in fact we can learn more from conflict than from pleasure. Without conflict we may just continue to sleep in life, without learning anything. So any unpleasant experience in life can be used as a teaching, an awakening, to bring wisdom. All spiritual masters, like Buddha or Christ, had painful experiences in life, through which they discovered what was important. It is not a matter of avoiding suffering but of going through it, working through it.

We need insight, and this cannot be given by anyone. It is within. What can we do in order to develop insight? We come here to the basic thing, which we call meditation. To meditate is to be simply aware of what is going on here and now; it is to find the capacity to live fully in the present, without being swayed by the past or the future. Insight does not always arise during a sitting period of meditation, but often comes afterwards. To meditate is in a way like a hen hatching eggs. During her period of sitting, the chickens do not emerge, but her sitting is necessary for them to come out later. If we sit and meditate without any expectation of insight, it will arise more easily. But if we sit with expectancy and impatience, disappointment and suffering arise.

The motive for meditating is to see, to look, to go through one's own conditioning, or to go through oneself. You see what kind of person you are, what your particular weaknesses, qualities and characteristics are, dominant or secondary, without having to be told by anyone, without being tested, interpreted or diagnosed. You can be your own analyst by looking into yourself, seeing yourself every moment. You are sitting, reading, talking with friends, going somewhere, being emotional — in any situation you can observe what is happening. When you see unpleasant things in yourself, a further reaction often arises — feelings of self-dislike, blame or guilt — but do not let this prevent you from continuing to look and *accept*. Without acceptance, seeing can become a form of self-torture and self-hatred, which can never lead to freedom.

It is a matter of seeing, without even categorising. If you say 'I am such-and-such a person', this creates a fixed idea. Then when you look at yourself you see the image held in your mind, instead of seeing yourself as you are at that moment. When you look at what is there, without ideas, you can see objectively. In that seeing there is balance. You are not emotionally involved or distracted or overwhelmed, yet you allow feeling to arise without attempting to ignore or repress it. Feeling arises naturally with intelligence and seeing — it is flowing all the time, and does not become negative unless it has been blocked or denied. So even if the feeling is unpleasant, there is no distortion unless it is not seen and accepted. If the intellect is overdeveloped, the energy of feeling is channelled into attitudes and judgments.

You can learn to meditate at any time, but it is essential that we have a proper period of training to begin with, because most people are not strong enough to look into themselves properly. This is a problem of fear, and of not understanding psychological processes. When you come across something which appears harmful and destructive, and you have no guidance, there may be a withdrawal and a reinforcement of fear so that further meditation is avoided. Or, on the other hand, there may be a blissful experience which the meditator would like to repeat, so that desire is strengthened and meditation is used as a substitute for drugs. Another pitfall (especially frequent in Hindu forms of meditation) is the wish for detachment, in which the mind finds relief in a suspended state dissociated from the flux and conflict of what is actually arising at every moment. Or refuge is sought in a higher being, God, or guru, which are trusted blindly to the exclusion of all else. Such a fixed state of belief brings a form of security which people long for, but lacks the flexibility upon which true freedom and contentment are based.

We have to allow continuous enquiry. This is not the compulsive questioning of the sceptic, but an open flow which can investigate everything without getting brainwashed. And a very important factor in this is *honesty*. Be honest with yourself, be frank, without trying to hide yourself, or prove you are right, or say that you are always wrong. To be honest is to be objective, to allow criticism without rejection. When we understand our habits and tendencies, and accept them, we shall be able to understand and accept others. This is the way in which harmony is established between individuals, who are neither naïve nor judgemental about each other.

What does it mean to be honest? First of all you may see that you are not honest, and if you look into this you will see the reasons why, not in theory but in practice. In working towards honesty we do not use ideas or principles, or philosophies, but we look at dishonesty in action. When the causes of dishonesty, and our need for deviation, are seen through, then honesty becomes easier and the direct path is taken. That is why, in the explanation of Nirvana, the Buddha expressed it in non-assertive terms: it is not the moon, not the sun, not the earth, not colour, and so on. Then the mind cannot hold on to a definite idea. Another way of doing this is through paradox, in which something is described as *both* this and that, apparently opposite and therefore impossible, but perfectly possible to the non-dualistic understanding.

This deep understanding creates inward flexibility. You move freely from point to point, and this is pleasant because movement is natural to the living. Flow also clears away obstacles and prevents stagnation, so that it is self-cleansing. If the mind becomes fixed, like water in a pond, it becomes polluted and can be dangerous, it cannot see beyond its own boundaries. But if it can move on, with awareness, it does not get stuck and remains young. The body may grow old, but the free mind, the mind with clear insight, is always young, and moves along the middle path.

There are two basic types of thinking. One is concentrative, which may be powerful but can also be dangerous because it cannot bend. It is linear and exclusive, rather than lateral and inclusive. It has strong attachment to support it, and lacks flexibility. At times we may need to use it for certain things, but it is unwise to do so for long, and in particular it should not be used with psychological problems, nor on a spiritual path. The other type of thinking we may call 'thinking from the heart'. Of course this does not mean the physical heart, which cannot think. What we call the heart is a centre of being — or just *being,* with no idea of centre. Thinking from the heart is open-ended perception of what is actually happening, without logic. It does not work from any point, angle, or principle, but passes through us from whatever arises, from the situation here and now. Being is not somewhere but anywhere, everywhere, and nowhere in particular, because it has no special place. Like the free man, the mind which thinks from the heart has no fixed abode. Its path is that of intuitive insight, the way of wisdom, and as the Buddha said, wisdom springs from meditation. It does not draw its power from the explosive energy of suppressed conflict, from the attempt to *make* the mind still, but from the nourishing flow of insight, when the mind becomes still naturally and the middle path of life can be lived.

II

THE URGENCY OF RADICAL CHANGE

Is CHANGE ESSENTIAL? If we look at the history of religion, there is a development of forms and symbols, with changes of emphasis which appear to match the needs of men according to their culture. In Buddhism, for instance, the first symbol we see is the Wheel of Truth, without the figure of man. The other early symbolism is the Empty Throne, under the Bodhi Tree where the Buddha is said to have been seated just before enlightenment. Then things changed, and although nobody has seen the Buddha in many centuries, there are many of his images throughout the world. These give people security and inspiration, as they want to look up to someone who is spiritually supreme. Buddha images were originally made to remind people of the historical Buddha and his example, but later on the symbol developed into an image of worship. It may be denied that all Buddhists worship the Buddha's image, but many do, who ask for help or who have a psychological need for worship.

Ideally, an image of the Buddha is used for strengthening our attention to his method and example, without identification. Identity is central to the ego, which longs for survival and cannot die away. We have the drive to be somebody or something. We cannot be alone, and would therefore prefer to be always surrounded by things or by people. It scares us to think of losing ourselves, but in fact it is chiefly the thought of this which is frightening — the experience itself is quite a different matter. Fear of annihilation of self is not just a modern phenomenon. At the time of the Buddha, the Hindus believed in a transcendental Self, and many rejected the Buddha's revolutionary teaching of *Anattā*, or Non-Self. This may be one of the major reasons why Buddhism did not endure in India, its birthplace, but spread to other countries whose social systems were not so dominated by ideas of spiritual hierarchy. In its more recent history, Buddhism sometimes puts the emphasis on a teaching of no-self, no-ego, stating that we are all already enlightened and would realise this immediately if we discarded the concept of self. But if ego were only a concept, it could be neutralised by the counter-concept of no-self, and our own experience soon tells us that this does not happen. What often does happen, unfortunately, is that people go about believing they are free from self, but this is contradicted by their own behaviour. Self is an extraordinarily deeply-rooted conditioning which continues to manifest in subtler forms up to the highest levels of spiritual development. We should not attempt to destroy it, but to see it.

If we look into our religions, into our beliefs, into our selves, we may see whether it is necessary for them to remain in a certain form. We human beings can rationalise and reform our systems, but usually in a normative and superficial way because it does not lead to profound change. External changes bring about further change, so our work is never done — we keep changing or adopting external forms, the shells of past teachings, without getting to the heart of the matter. We have to realise that *radical change within us* is the most important change, from which other changes flow and from which discernment arises. If there is no such change we remain in the process of becoming and never understand our true being. What do we mean by radical change? It is not a matter of replacing one system with another, of creating new isms, new schools of thought, or of introducing new conceptual structures. What is it, then? By indicating what it is not, we may be able to see what it is.

The letting go of that which is false is the only truly creative action. How do we know what is false? How can we judge? Do we have to rely on our own views, or can we come to an understanding of falsity? This is our biggest question. True judgment of what is false does not spring from what we have been told, or from conditioned opinion, but from insight into the nature of things which seeks no confirmation from other people's beliefs. Usually we want support from someone who 'knows', because we have no direct knowledge of what we perceive. External authority makes the mind weak, because it encourages it not to find out for itself. It has been trained in this way — information is given from an external source, and has been for centuries. Even in schools which transmit 'higher truths', knowledge in the form of subtle ideas indoctrinates the mind because it does not arise spontaneously from the purified vision of the pupil himself. Literature often perpetuates the teaching of such secondhand inspiration without showing the student how to experience at first hand the source from which the original seer received his revelation. Any idea, however inspired, takes a form which the mind may find difficulty in relinquishing, so that purification of mental centres remains incomplete. For a very long time, people have accumulated teachings and beliefs; the habit of wanting to be told goes deep. Others, to whom knowledge gives power, use it to control or mystify those who seek the truth, instead of revealing the path. They cannot reveal the essential, because they have not seen it, being too occupied with substitutes. So they recommend the false, without realising fully what they are doing.

We have to be careful, particularly with ourselves. We are dangerous beings in an unenlightened state, and we have to recognise this. At the same time, we have unique possibilities. There are different factors working within us: destructive, deluded elements which endanger a vicious circle, and constructive, intuitive elements which give rise to a virtuous circle. According to the balance of these elements, the circle can change into a spiral. The first step needed is an understanding of ourselves as we are at present, otherwise the striving for change will be a waste of time and energy.

One does not become enlightened through ego plans for enlightenment. Why is this? It is because ego is concerned with Goal (with concepts of will, achievement, mastery, gain and happiness) rather than Path (with its facts of patience, ego-loss, and acceptance of certain sufferings) which give rise to Liberation, not in the ego sense of freedom but of Equanimity. If awareness is given to the next step, then the next, with diligence (the last word uttered by the Buddha during his lifetime) with the right method and direction, the destination will be reached automatically without preconception. But an eye to the future without insight into the present is like a climber trying to leap to the summit without attending to his immediate surroundings and route. If precipitation methods are used (such as fixed concentration instead of attentive awareness, or chemical changes artificially induced by intensive exercises or drugs) spiritual experiences may occur but may not be transformative, because the self is suspended rather than worked through. There is detachment rather than equanimity, dissociation instead of liberated relationship. Experiences of enlightenment are very different from Realisation.

Many of us find it difficult to make progress in meditation because we want to achieve an experience, or hope that something will happen to us so that each time our meditation will be 'better'. We have to work without expecting results, without focusing our minds upon any goal of enlightenment. Give up these things; don't care about success — but care for the action, the doing with awareness at every moment. We are taking a journey, and it does not matter if we are certain of our destination or not. In ordinary journeys we may know where we are going and what we shall meet on the way, but in our spiritual journey through life this cannot be so. Faith does not mean certainty, but the acceptance of uncertainty, which requires courage but lays the foundation of liberation. If we allow the possibility that there may be no such thing as reaching our destination, then we may discover where the truth really lies.

If we hold on to the idea of a goal, tension arises. We think that we work in order to 'produce' Nirvana. If Nirvana could be produced, it would be a product we could easily sell! We need to change our attitude towards enlightenment and allow the dissolution of conditioning which for so long has appeared to support us, but in fact prevents our real stability. Since we are at present ego-orientated our work may at first come from spiritual ambition, but because the self is not consistent we sometimes find ourselves in a situation of choice. That is a crucial moment, when the possibility of radical change arises, and if we take the opportunity of changing direction at that moment we shall find more and more choice later on. However, if we ignore or avoid such opportunities, they will recur less often. Fewer crossroads will be encountered, and we shall fall more deeply asleep on the motorway of unconscious behaviour.

Psychological sleep insulates us from the importance of change, and we believe that all is well, until suffering is our Awakener. In order to see what is wrong, what is false, one has to wake up, otherwise one will continue to believe 'I am conscious of myself, my actions, my surroundings, my world', without realising one is still asleep. A person dreams that he is awake. Ordinary consciousness gives false information when in the state of psychological dreaming. You may ask who can say 'I am awake'. There is no need for anyone to say it. In the awakened state there is charity and silence, without concern for acknowledgment, and without discrimination between anybody or anything because these are irrelevant. The mind no longer adheres to duality, or distinguishes between the superficial and the profound.

Do we realise that our house is on fire? In one of the Buddha's sermons it is said that he referred to all things as 'burning'. If we do not see this we shall not be moved to take action before the situation deteriorates further, our choices dwindle, and the fire of our desire bars our path. The 'I' thinks it will reach happiness through the fulfilment of its desires. Many of its wishes appear completely harmless, but the state of ignorance is in fact dangerous; our back is turned, and sooner or later when physical and mental sufferings arise we shall have no insight into their source. Our energies will be spent in a desperate retreat instead of a radical change, and from a position of stress and defence there is less choice.

The 'I' does not wish to see that its house is burning, because if it realised this it could no longer live there and would be forced to take action. The sense of urgency comes when we see the danger of our situation, when we begin to wake up. Then change occurs on its own accord, not because of our desire to force a change but because of our seeing. What is the difference between seeing and perception? Perception is conditioned by past experience, which causes us to recognise something with reference to what is known. Can we see without recognition? This would be the sight of a child who sees something for the first time, without preconceived ideas. But soon he wishes to relate it to knowledge, and asks his parents 'What is it?' Is it possible for us to see things without a context? To look into another person's face without having any concept of a human being or a face, and to see what is there? It is a kind of death of the mind, through which intuitive perception can occur, without images — pure seeing. As the Buddha said twenty-five centuries ago: what is seen is only seeing. We can understand this if we are really curious. This matter of seeing is important because, in a way, seeing is knowing and includes other faculties such as hearing. It is not ordinary hearing with the ears, but lies behind all the senses. The truth of seeing does not lie in the explanation of its processes and structures, so do not get stuck in words. Practise letting the mind go, and you will experience the great sound that lies behind silence. Silence has power — that is why it has been said that silence is eloquent speech.

Give up everything you have, without asking how. If you start waiting about for the how, there will be no end to it. The answer to how is *now* : look with attention, and you will see what happens. That attention has everything you need, bringing the golden key to seeing. This key cannot be grasped, but it can be used. The Buddha's whole teaching is concerned with *not* holding on, but making use of everything, like using a raft to cross the river of life and relinquishing it on reaching the other shore. He compared the attempt to grasp an idea with trying to grasp a poisonous snake — if you grab its tail it will bite you, or if you hold on to its middle it can still bite you. How do you grasp the snake without allowing it to bite you? How do you grasp an idea without it holding on to you? A certain technique is essential, by which we take hold of the snake firmly by its head, so that it cannot control or harm us. In this way you can listen to everyone, whether famous or not, even a child; you can listen to everything, even the trees and the grass, without accumulating memories; you can let ideas flow and drop away, leaving you to travel alone, freely and lightly.

Is it possible to change the whole structure of our selves, the processes of our thinking and perceiving? We should not concern ourselves at first with external forms but with inner qualities. Only when we look into ourselves can we change, and this takes place by itself, without our concentrating upon such change. If we look only at what is there, we can put aside secondhand teachings without carrying them about in our minds in the hope that they will change us. This would be like holding the snake to your breast! We are free to read scriptures and to discuss them, neither blindly accepting them as the truth, nor being aloof and sceptical. Do not quote the Buddha as ultimate authority — perhaps he did not say it at all! His work of reform lay in deconditioning the mind, not in accumulating more ideas. He did not teach from theory, but from his own seeing, and we can follow his path in this life without worrying about next life, or next week.

Anxiety about the future robs us of the energy with which we could deal with it, as well as spoiling the present — which is actually all there *is*. It is sometimes relevant for the intellect to plan ahead, but to mix this with emotional anticipation is like an engine racing out of gear. This is a habit which usually originates in childhood, when parents promise pleasures or threaten punishments to come, thus displacing their children's natural awareness of the present into the future. Threatening possibilities are particularly harmful because, unlike actuality, they can rarely be dealt with directly — the drive towards action, with its psychological and physical states of preparation, is in a vacuum. Potential is therefore linked with powerlessness, which increases anxiety. Even the anticipation of pleasure is not as harmless as it may at first appear, because it is an artificial stimulation of mood, detracting from the flow of attention to the present. It is a poor substitute for spontaneous contentment, and because it is again not based on what is actual, its fulfilment also remains potential — and therefore insatiable. When a society teaches its members to lose contact with the present, they thus lose both power and satisfaction in their true sense. In some countries this has led to an apathetic population; in others the combination of impotence and dissatisfaction has led to great frustration and suffering, either expressed in aggression or escaped through fantasy. You hear some people say we should not be deprived of our fantasies in this drab world, but they do not see how unreality and illusion engender poverty, ugliness, futility, and continued avoidance. Their view is encouraged by exploiters and accepted by unconscious people, so perpetuating the cycle of what Buddhists call 'unskilful states' : greed, hate, and delusion.

In spiritual work, look after the present, taking responsibility for your actions, and the future will change. That is why it has been said that the end lies within the beginning. Work has to be done here and now. If we change our orientation and look at what is actually here, Reality will not be just a concept and we shall enter the stream of Nirvana, which is not a static state but the flow of life *as it is,* a moving reality. It is not something 'out there', but is anywhere, or nowhere in particular. It is not an abode of bliss, but lies within life itself and can be experienced at any moment. It is not an elevated state of being, so do not wonder what you will be in Nirvana. You will be what you are — nothing special. Do not plan what you will be doing, because you will do nothing — it will all be done. Do not think about what you will get — the 'I' will not be there to demand anything. All that is needed will be there, as it already is but we have not realised it because we believe we need something else. In turning towards what we think we want, we miss what we really need. The answer is so close to us that we cannot see it. Look to the present and you will begin to understand the truth about 'I' and about Nirvana.

III

MEDITATION: THE TECHNIQUE
FOR CHANGING PERSONALITY

BEFORE WE GO into the details of our subject, let us look at what meditation means. This word is used in various ways by different schools. To me meditation is the way, the means, by which we sharpen our awareness — an objective, non-interfering awareness — and develop our insight. These two tools of awareness and insight enable a mediator to go through himself and come to awakening or enlightenment consciousness. This is the universal consciousness, for it does not belong to anybody, it is not confined to any particular place, but it can be found and realised by individuals. Simply stated, meditation is to be aware, to be alert, to be awake.

Most of the time we are asleep, even in our normal waking life. This sleep has several aspects. During the day our waking consciousness is operating. Sometimes we go into daydreaming, fantasies, restlessness or trance with our eyes open. When we are tired at night, we go to sleep. This unawakened consciouness operates to keep life going and continuous. We may call it the life continuum consciousness. Through all these levels we sleep with what we have, with what we have accumulated, without knowing what we are or where we are going.

Meditation is the way for us to take a journey through our life and see all its aspects : how life continues to exist and how we function in daily life. Is it possible to go beyond our conditioned consciousness, beyond the programmed patterns that move us through the day? Without meditation you cannot really get into the depth of life. You stay with superficial things and miss the chance to find your inner treasure. Sometimes we may think that life is too difficult and so full of trouble and pain, engendered by negative experiences, that it is not worth living. Then we might do something destructive to ourselves or to life, and that is unwise action. This feeling of depression arises when we lack the means to look and go into ourselves, to experience all the levels of existence and the different states of consciousness.

26

Particularly for the people of the East, meditation became the main technique to arrive at enlightenment as the Buddha and other religious masters and sages did. And not only in the East, but in the West too, meditation or contemplation has been used as the means for realisation, for experiencing the ultimate goal of religious life. How can meditation help us today, as modern Westerners, to change our consciousness? If we meditate, do we have to sit in a very formal posture at a certain time? Or can it be practised in every-day living? Meditation does exist in such sitting *and* it exists in all aspects of life if we understand how to apply it. We can see that formal sitting in meditation is essential for training. We need a certain period of practice in order to be able to apply our ideals and to get into what we would like to develop. If we do not have time to train ourselves, then we will find it extremely difficult to put our principles into practice during our daily life. We should follow both the training system of formal sitting and the application of the meditation principle to daily practice. Together, these two are very effective.

How does meditation affect the personality? For us the personality may be the main concern, for many of us experience problems of personality disorder or disturbance. We do not feel easy in life or in work; we do not feel at home with our environment or with anything we do or experience. The personality becomes negative and destructive, unable to give happiness and harmony in living. Let us look into this personality. What do we see? Is it only physical process or is there something here to do with the mind? The personality is the expression, the manifestation of both the inner and outer qualities of our nature. What we are in the outside world represents what we have within us and how we became what we are. The heavier attitudes, tendencies and habits are surely the inner conditions which we have developed from early childhood up to the present moment. If we can look at our personality, examine our attitudes and habits of feeling and acting, then we will be able to find what is wrong and where we are not in harmony with ourselves. This understanding does not come from knowledge gained from books or other people, but through direct observation and the direct awareness we practise and develop.

When we are in a constant movement of observation, we can have that clarity of seeing and understanding which is called *insight*. Insight means seeing within. We see through the inner eye of wisdom, not through the framework of our knowledge. Knowledge does not help very much because it is in the head and does not go to the heart. When we have insight we have no distorting process interfering. This insight becomes the liberating factor that creates order and harmony. We can become balanced and integrated with our bodily functions and movements, with our emotions and consciousness.

How can we bring about the unity of all these parts that we seem to be? First of all, you must start with yourself as you are, not with an idea of what you should be or would like to be. If you follow the idea, you create a gap, a gap between reality and fantasy that can cause conflict. If you cannot sense this gap, then what you should be becomes only the idea. This is why it is very difficult to find the harmony of personality. So you start from where you are, from what you can see of yourself. You begin to look, to observe all your activities, all your conditioning, abilities and potentialities, and the powers you may have within you. Curiosity motivates this search. You do not have any preconceived faith or belief but a great curiosity to look and find out if there is a goodness in human beings. You do not accept the ideas or views of others. Leave all those things alone. Say rather, 'Now I am going to find out. I am going to look.' Then you begin to apply your awareness. When you go out into the world and when you sit and meditate, keep your attention steady and look. Apply this awareness to whatever you come across — people, books, nature. You look with a clear and silent mind which brings about the intelligence of understanding. The thing which is not right will not be taken in, and the thing which is right, that which is growing within you, will be brought out. In this way awareness becomes the interflow between the outer and inner world, helping you to function positively in life. Then all the barriers standing in the way of life's flow, what we call ego, ego fiction, ego fixation or defences, will be gradually overcome and finally disappear. Awareness can then function through more and more of our experience. Objective non-interfering awareness is the most important factor in meditation, for it develops personality and changes consciousness.

Now let me talk about some stages of insight. In Buddhism there are four levels of consciousness. During meditation each level is being purified by the process of awareness and insight. This creates the possibility of coming to the next level of consciousness. The first level deals with the world of experience, the waking state of existence. This kind of consciousness is run by two circles, the vicious and the virtuous. It creates conflict within itself all the time. The vicious and virtuous circles form one of the aspects of a system. In Buddhism the individual is formed of five aggregates : the aggregates of the body, of feeling, perception, consciousness, and of mental formations or habit tendencies. All of these form vicious and virtuous circles. The virtuous circle represents all the positive, constructive qualities of life : wisdom, awareness of the tendency to do good, the tendency to avoid the extreme way of acting, living and feeling, and the tendency to become mentally healthy, to be sane. The vicious circle represents all the negative and destructive qualities within us : the tendency to do evil, the tendency to become inactive and lazy, mentally inert. The vicious circle fosters an unproductive personality which has downers, uncertainty and fear. These two circles create conflict, the basic conflict of life. If we do not understand how they operate within us, we lose balance. We human beings cannot be completely free from both circles, nevertheless we have balance, which will keep us at the human level. The virtuous circle will encourage us and give a certain direction for us to move towards the truth of life. That is why we have the urge to search, to look for something deep and to become liberated. We all look for the same thing : to come to total freedom in this life.

Sometimes we are held back by the vicious circle. If we are aware of how it comes to stand in our way, we can move beyond it as the Buddha did. According to the story, he went out of the city at night and came across Māra, the evil tempter in Buddhism. Māra said : 'Where are you going? You know you will soon become an emperor. Why leave the palace?' The Buddha stopped his horse and listened. He understood it all, 'Ah, Māra', and went on. He did not say anything to Māra, he just went on, acknowledging, 'That is Māra, the vicious circle.' He had already given up his palace and the thought of his wife and child. On the day of enlightenment the Buddha was once tempted by Māra; and when he was aware of his aim, he overcame Māra and continued his meditation until dawn when he became enlightened.

Even after becoming enlightened, the Buddha was occasionally tempted by Māra. This means that the vicious circle still exists in the ordinary consciousness. Since the enlightened man has pure awareness and awakening, he knows what is happening on the surface. When the Buddha was tempted by Māra, he would just say, 'Oh Māra, I know you.' (He was quite friendly with Māra.) Say, 'Oh Māra, I know you', and Māra cannot do anything.

So the primary step into insight is insight into duality. Duality arises first of all between the body and mind. We look to see how the mind functions and how the body functions. In this area, books on psychology may help us understand how the mind works, but in order to see it for ourselves, we must put aside all book knowledge and information. Relying on your experience, you will understand in depth.

The next stage of insight opens our understanding of conditionality. By observing our thoughts and emotions, we are able to see that each of them is conditioned by something else. Thought is not a thing in itself. If you look superficially, you may say, 'Oh, it is only a thought, a single, isolated event.' No. Look again. Do not try to put on any interpretation or come to an easy conclusion. That is a kind of self-deception. Just look to see as clearly and deeply as possible. Is the thought conditioned by other things? Are there underlying conditions, underlying causes or motives behind the purpose of thinking? Perhaps you may be able to see how the thought connects itself with other thoughts or with the very ground of thinking. Look deeper and deeper with this inquiring mind and be careful that it is not noisy. You must not try to frame the word. The inquiring mind must be silent, though it can use very precise questions about what you are observing. After putting a question, the mind becomes quiet, looks very attentively, deeply and thereby gains clarity. This process clears away the cloud of unknowing, the cloud of accepted 'knowledge' and fear. All barriers pass away and the deep understanding of insight into conditionality appears. So at this second stage your mind becomes very steady and clear. This inner stability shows in a new level of perception and awareness. Consciousness is wakeful and restful, yet it still has a sense of form. Even though it is no longer very strong, there is the perception of form and of names and the perception of ideas.

The next two steps of insight are connected with the integrated and harmonised functioning of intellect and insight. To come to these stages, we first learn to think objectively. Thinking objectively involves us in the subject/object relationship. Instead of thinking from the subject, the ego centre, you think from the object, from the situation. You are able to step outside of yourself and see from another perspective. Then you will come to the third stage of insight where you see into the different characteristics of existence.

At the third level you begin to make inferences from the changes, in bodily functions, in feelings, thoughts and emotions. Whatever you see reveals its changing nature, demonstrating that nothing is permanent. When there is insight into impermanence or 'anicca', you can develop the attitude of being free and detached. The ego becomes supple and loses its grip on any idea or emotion. You begin to perceive some calmness, a lightness of the body and clarity of the head. Sometimes you may come across light, a very bright light. Some call it hallucination. It is a mental picture, the discharge of the body and mind. Many things will discharge at this stage. For certain periods you may also feel very joyful and peaceful. This bliss will not last for very long but comes occasionally. At other times, the things you know or have read but do not understand completely will become clear. You will say, 'Oh, that's the meaning'. Finally at this stage you come to a strong confidence in the path of awareness and feel deep gratitude towards your instructor, parents or others who are close to you.

When you are at this point of insight, the personality begins to change and move towards a more positive and constructive existence in the world. Consciousness is being developed and purified. At the peak of this level there is no form, but a perception of infinity, of the vastness and depth of things. Seeing becomes very subtle. Sometimes it is difficult to say whether there is perception or not since form is absent. When there is no form, the act of recognising and judging cannot function for they are both dependent on form and concepts. So at this third level perception becomes subtle and deep, yet not completely free.

The fourth level of consciousness is called awakened or enlightened, where there is illumination, clarity and alertness — perfect alertness with non-verbal insight. This awakened consciousness gives a freedom that is not connected to any form of emotion or with like and dislike. Freedom is just being free. If you sit, you are free to sit; if you walk, you are free to walk. There is no uneasiness, no anxiety, no disturbance. When you wake up fully, you see everything clearly. You are not distracted, because you see everything as it is. You are not concerned with any elements or images of what you see. Buddhism regards this true, luminous consciousness as intrinsic to every human being. The sense impressions that intrude upon us becloud it. If we do not establish awareness at the doors of the senses, we are left without a keeper, when destructive elements enter our consciousness making it impure and defiled. Our task is to cleanse it away through meditation. Then we can get into the creative aspect of living where we find energy, wakefulness and the treasures of our life.

You may still come across dualistic experiences (good/bad, constructive/destructive, negative/positive), but that is part of life. You know that anything that comes to you will only stay temporarily. Nothing, neither good nor bad, can be with you forever. So you are not attached, you do not grasp and hold on. You are also not detached in the sense of escaping from the reality of life. You will become realistic, looking at life, seeing it for what it is. You have learnt to accept whatever arises and to practise acceptance in action, not in the idea. Beliefs, doubt and uncertainty are replaced by understanding and seeing. This acceptance is not what some people, only superficially acquainted with Eastern terminology, call Karma. They think they are practising acceptance when, in fact, they are merely being passive. 'Oh, it is my karma, I cannot do anything about it.' That person accepts anything coming to him, so he stops looking and becomes inactive. He loses insight into his situation. The way of meditation tells us to observe with awareness any situation we come across so that we can learn and remain flexible, flowing. When you feel fixated, you seem to get nowhere; you are uncomfortable and unable to function properly. Some people experience this state as ageing, madness or boredom. Now, what can we do?

Vipassana Meditation will say, look at this state of being fixed and see how you block yourself. What is happening right now? If you go into the present completely, you will see the facts and the truth of what is. Then you move on. You dissolve the problem in the light of clarity, the light of awareness. When you have the means to deal with yourself, you become your own psychotherapist. You need not say, 'Oh, I am a psychotherapist. I will look into myself.' No, the label is not important, but the ability to look is, for this looking will bring about insight. Insight will peer into a situation, penetrate, and break it. The barriers are cleared away and we can flow on with life. There is joy and happiness; there is sorrow and pain. We accept them all. Pain and sorrow in life can often awaken our wisdom. When we are too happy, we can be lost in the happiness and gain no wisdom. We should regard unpleasant or unfortunate situations in life as spiritual lessons for growth and maturity. They test us to see whether we are strong enough, whether we are free or not.

Life will surely provide situations for testing, otherwise you cannot know that you have grown and become fully mature. Even when you come to enlightened consciousness, you may sometimes be put in a situation which will test whether you can apply awakened consciousness to living in the conditioned world. If someone says, 'Yes, I have become enlightened. I live in the forest in a cave and see no human being', he cannot really claim that he is completely free. So put him to the test: put him into society and see how he reacts. Is the ego still functioning negatively or destructively? If so, he needs the world as a teacher in order to grow. The Buddha said that the enlightened man abides in the world like a lotus growing in muddy water. The lotus stands above the water, undefiled. The enlightened man can live and grow in the conditioned world without becoming its victim. His consciousness is always awakened, so he has alertness and understanding, with energy to live, energy to work.

When he works, his consciousness is not distracted, so his energy is not dissipated and he does not get tired easily. Tiredness is a mental attitude towards life or a particular situation. But the enlightened man does not follow an attitude. Through meditation, he has cleared out his mind. So meditation gives us the opportunity to become aware of our attitudes, of the patterns that shape our personality. Once insight has shown us how these function, we will be able to change our relationship to ourselves, to other people and to the world around us.

IV

THE PROBLEM OF LIVING

IF BUDDHISM HAS to do with life, with the happiness and peace of people, the problem of living must be understood. Do we have problems in life, in living? I am sure all of us have in one way or another and it is very essential to look into these problems of living; it does not matter how many we have. Perhaps we don't want to go into all the details of all the different problems which different people have, but it is essential for all of us to look into the one main basic problem. That is the problem of living itself. Living is a problem and perhaps we may use the Buddhist word 'dukkha' — dukkha is the problem of living. If we do not understand the problem of living, or if we do not understand that in life there are both suffering and pleasure, and that both the constructive and destructive elements are operating in life, we will not understand why we have conflict.

Conflict arises because of the operation of the two opposite elements or, in other words, the two circles, the vicious and the virtuous circle. If we are free from both circles we go beyond concepts and then there is no problem; but so long as we are living within the circles — the Buddhist word is Samsāra — then problems cannot be avoided. The more we try to avoid problems the more we have. So the best thing is to face the problem as it is. We have to see it. So if we look into this problem of living we may say that life is not always pleasant and not always unpleasant; sometimes life is enjoyable, inviting, appealing and sometimes life is horrible, miserable, full of conflict and contradiction. We have to accept that fact. If we don't accept the facts of life it is not possible to understand the problem of living. Perhaps we are trying to avoid the destructive, unpleasant side of life: we try to be good, we try to be happy, we try to be awakened, we try to be enlightened, we try to be many good things, and that trying to be or to become something, itself creates the problem.

We all build up images, images of ourselves, because we have all the information available to us to know what kind of person it is who is enlightened, what kind of a person is awakened, what kind of person is good; we have all the information available and because of this knowledge we try to form the image as a goal, an ideal, and we look for that. Perhaps when we go to someone who we feel is enlightened or awakened, then we form an image of that person and perhaps put that person in a very important position, give him a very high image, and then get stuck there. It is very interesting to see how we form or create images in life. So long as we do not understand how we create these images for our own security, our own certainty, then we do not accept insecurity, uncertainty. Perhaps the word faith as generally used is just the expression of that uncertainty. When we accept the uncertainty we are strong enough to experiment with, to explore, life. It does not matter how difficult it is but when we walk along a path, when we live our life clinging to certainty and security, then we can never experiment with all aspects of life, and inwardly, psychologically we are in conflict with ourselves and with other people, and in conflict with life itself because life has to flow. Life is always in a state of flux; it can never stop. So when the flow of life never stops we try to direct its movement into a certain direction according to the information we believe we have, and then life is put in a state of chaos, of disorderliness.

Things in the world and in life have order within themselves but we do not believe that because we demand a certain knowledge, we must hear a certain person talking about it first before we can believe that it is so. And that is the problem of living again, because we don't take the initiative. We cannot take the initiative because we are full of fear and uncertainty and anxiety. So what shall we do? We have to understand ourselves as we are and first of all we have to accept ourselves as we are. It doesn't matter if people give you an image, because people have their own opinions, people have the right to believe, to speak, in the way they think is right and they will think and speak according to their own conditioning. But if you know yourself as you are then you know what you are doing and then there is no problem in living. I don't mean that there is no difficulty. There may be some difficulty in dealing with other people, in having relationships with people, but that is a part of life. It cannot be avoided, it has to be understood, and by going through any difficulties, any troubles, we see more about ourselves. We gain deeper understanding of ourselves. So insight is deepening itself by going through any experience, provided we know what we are doing.

Suffering plays a very important part in life, but we do not accept it. We do not want to suffer and because of not wanting to suffer we suffer psychologically. We are killing each other, not physically, but killing each other by thinking about others in a negative way, even by using harsh, disharmonious words we are killing and hurting each other. But that is a part of life, and we have to understand that we are killing each other. If we don't accept that then we can never understand ourselves. We have to know why we kill each other. We kill one another in our way of living, in our work, as when we try to climb to the top we kick away other people, so we are killing those people. This world of competition is full of killing. Buddhism is against any form of killing: killing by words, killing by action, by force. And if we look closely we can see that we are in a state of uncertainty and insecurity. Thus it is very essential for all of us to look at ourselves, to take full responsibility for our actions, or, in other words, to look at the present to see life as it is.

Is it possible for any one of us to look into life without having any concepts, without having any background knowledge that life should be such-and-such, according to the Buddha, according to Christ, according to any religious master? Are we free to look into life without having any concepts, any reference? If we can do this it is much easier to understand life. But when we look into life within the context of some teaching, we are not looking into life at all, we are reflecting upon life according to the teachings, with this second-hand knowledge. This second-hand knowledge becomes the greatest barrier to clear seeing, to enlightenment itself. We may say it is not possible for any one of us not to have second-hand knowledge in order to know or to see, and we may say this because of insecurity. The Buddha made it clear that standing on this shore of life is full of dangers, full of fears and uncertainties. That is very true, but we have to recognise this state of being, this state of existence. If we do not recognise it then we do not accept it as it is. How can we make the step towards the other shore? Yes, we have second-hand knowledge, and we are happy using that knowledge to discuss or talk about our situation, without seeing it or without understanding the real situation within ourselves. And that may be a waste of time and a waste of energy.

Why do we suffer? Perhaps it is easy to understand physical suffering because of pain or discomfort. When we sit here for some time our body becomes uncomfortable and we feel it is not easy to sit; we would like to get up, to move. Or if we are sitting here and our mind is elsewhere, thinking about something else, perhaps some problem, or thinking about what we should do tomorrow, then we do not have happiness and in a way we suffer because we think that when we come here to listen to the lecture we should have peace of mind. But we don't have it, which is unfortunate, and we suffer again. So we must look into our situation and find out why we suffer. Is suffering something very real or is it only the ignorance due to illusion going on in the mind or in the body? It is difficult to say what is real and what is unreal. It is not a matter for speculation, but for seeing, understanding. What is real cannot be put into words. The more we try to describe the real the more complicated it becomes.

It is a matter of seeing. But *how* can I see? We always look for the *how*; the *how* becomes the greatest problem. Perhaps if we just drop this problem of how, and then look at everything with full attention, now at this moment, then things will become simpler, easier. When the mind demands 'How?', it can never come to simplicity, and that is the problem again, the problem of living. We are not free from the techniques, the methods, from the means by which we see. Let's simply look into ourselves now, not tomorrow, not the next moment. I think we know that we suffer, but do we know why? We suffer because we cannot get what we want, we cannot succeed in our work, in our life; we cannot fulfil our desires and ambitions, and so we suffer. When we suffer we can see that we are completely dependent, psychologically, on the idea, the ideal, of success. Suppose you want to be a very successful person but cannot see how to be successful. You create psychological dependence on success. You find it very difficult to live a simple life because the mind is always demanding success. So we just drop the dependence, drop the idea of success, and look at our actions, the doing, how we do things. We look at it and then we don't care for success or failure. It doesn't matter. Sometimes you fail, sometimes you succeed. That is part of life. Don't try to complicate it. Then we will flow into the order of life, the order of the universe, the order of living.

When the problem of living has been understood there is no suffering, particularly no psychological suffering. But this does not mean that we do not think about problems, about suffering. We do think about these in order to see all aspects of different kinds of suffering. We do not think in the sense of reacting to the problems, or responding to problems according to certain conditions, but we think in the sense of looking into the problems, bringing the heart with us to see the problems with full attention. Then our thinking is without words. Normal thinking is full of words, full of pictures and images and in general there is no thinking which is free from words, but if we go deeper into this thinking which is free from words, the thinking from the heart, we will understand that this kind of thinking operates very closely with intuitive understanding. That is why the Buddha put the two categories on the eightfold path, right understanding and right thinking, into the form of wisdom. Wisdom has two aspects, thinking and understanding, and it goes with the heart. Not the physical heart, but heart; it doesn't matter if you call it the spiritual heart or give it another name. In the heart there is love, understanding, and freedom. When people do not feel they do not have a heart. You come across things in life and you don't feel for them. You come across other people and you never feel for them, or you come across the grass, the water, the table, or you go to your kitchen or go anywhere. If you don't have heart you don't have feeling and if you don't feel for anything you come across then surely you have no heart. When you have heart you have very deep feeling for something, you have love for it and then your action flows. That is very natural and there is nothing to prevent it, so we must look into ourselves and see whether we have heart or if we just have head. When the head is fully occupied, full of thoughts and ideas, then the heart disappears; the head becomes so big, so large, that the heart cannot come into being. We have to look into this to see for ourselves the suffering in life.

We may say that suffering arises because of attachment, because of desire, because of ignorance. If there is no ignorance there is no suffering and the problem of living can be solved by seeing, understanding life fully as it is. That is real Buddhism. The Buddha never tried to teach anyone to substitute something else for suffering by saying that you must seek pleasure or joy or anything else so that you can overcome suffering. No, the Buddha was straightforward in saying that we must see suffering as it is, that is the way to overcome it, to be free. But it may be said that if we have to look into the suffering of life we will all have pessimistic views, pessimistic attitudes towards life and then we will not be happy. Again that is another opinion. Why should we be pessimistic or optimistic? Why care for it too much? If we see things as they are it doesn't matter if other people say you are pessimistic or optimistic. These two categories will not come to be if we see things as they are. We will become realistic and see the world as it is. We don't have to have any pessimistic or optimistic views about life or about the world. Is it true that there is suffering going on in life, particularly psychological suffering, and why do we have this psychological suffering? Is it because of external conditions, because society is not good enough for us to live in or is it because of our own inner conditions and because of our ability or inability to manage our relationships within ourselves and in the world? Or is it the conforming to certain idealistic principles that creates the problem of psychological suffering? When something opposite to what we believe, to what we know, comes to be, we suffer or when the image we look up to changes or goes into another direction we also suffer. Now you have no image — how fortunate!

It is very interesting to look into this psychological suffering. If we do this then we can see how unreal it is, but when you don't see it, it becomes very real in your thinking, in your perceiving, and you suffer tremendously. Are we satisfied with second-hand knowledge or do we aim to get first-hand knowledge for ourselves? First-hand knowledge can come to be in every moment of living by looking at, by watching, every situation in life with full attention. Nothing more. And that is not the beginning or the end; that is the doing, the living. Don't ask how you can come to the time when you can stop looking with attention. That is nonsense. You want to stop somewhere and that is the trouble. We want to build up something, to produce something, to protect ourselves. The 'me' wants to be protected. If anything can be produced in order that we may be protected that thing is illusion. Nirvana cannot be produced. If we could produce Nirvana, we could sell it! Many people want Nirvana, but it cannot be produced. The best thing we can do is to realise this, to see it — or, in other words, to enter the stream of Nirvana. Very interesting that the Buddha used the word stream — the stream of Nirvana. In a way Nirvana is flowing, but it is flowing in Samsāra, in the circle of life; or perhaps it may lie beyond these circles, and without working through, going through, the circles we can never come to the stream of Nirvana. We might wish to put the circles aside and go straight to Nirvana, but nobody can do that — the only way is to work through and it is a very painful way, but it is a way. A person might say 'Oh, I can go to Nirvana directly without having any suffering, without working through', but that person is deceiving himself. The problem of living has to be understood. This is the problem of how we live our life.

Again the question of *how*. How we live our life means by which *way* we live our life; by conforming, or by taking initiative, looking into life, living it without conforming to any ideas or knowledge. When we conform to ideas, knowledge or experience, beliefs, faiths or religions, surely we build up an image of life and that image of life is like a mirage. We stick to it, we hold on to this image. Then we go further and further away from life, from living, but if we go into it we see what life is, what living is. What do we mean by living? What does it mean to live so that everyone of us does not think about theories, but finds out actually what it means to live. Perhaps we think that to live is to have pleasure, to have joy, to have happiness, to be free from any kind of suffering, misery, agony or trouble, but if we have such an idea our life becomes divided and fragmented because we go from one extreme to another and never find the middle way. The middle way is not the way of asceticism or the way of hedonism. The middle way is not very easy to find and to walk along. When we conform to a certain idea, perhaps the idea that we are Buddhists, we say that Buddhism teaches the middle way and so if I am a Buddhist I walk along the middle way. Perhaps not; I may walk along a very extreme way if I hold on to the teaching without looking at the facts. The Buddha made it clear that the teaching is not for holding on to, but for using as a raft, a boat, to cross over the sea of life. Attachment in any form brings about suffering. Attachment to the teaching of the Buddha, or attachment to the Buddha in order to protect him, brings about suffering. Perhaps sometimes when people say something unpleasant about the Buddha we may be angry and think we have to protect the Buddha, or if we are Christian and people say something unpleasant about Christ we have to prevent it and defend Christ.

We all have self-defensive activities in life. We may appreciate the idea of no-self, no-ego, ego-loss, but our behaviour and our actions are the contrary to what we know. We have a self-image, we have plans for life, we have plans for enlightenment. Some people may plan that in about twenty years' time they will come to enlightenment. That is a form of self-image and so the no-self is not practised. We have to look into ourselves. Why do we not do that? We have to go through all aspects of life, through our ignorance, through our attachments and desires. When we see it, it is very easy to drop it, but when we do not see it we cannot drop it. We are not strong enough to drop it because fear is very strong. Fear has a close connection to attachment and ignorance. Suffering is a form of ignorance, nothing else. When a person is really wise he can never suffer, but sees the suffering in life, in the world, without committing himself to suffering. You may think this is not possible. It is not possible to our conditioned mind, but to the mind which is free from conditioning impossibility has no meaning. There is no tendency to think in a dualistic way.

Life has so many things to give and life has so many ways of punishing, if we like to think of it in that way; so rewards and punishment go hand in hand in life. Unless we go through and work through until we come to the completely steady state of being, life fluctuates, it goes to one circle and then the other circle, but by going through the circles we will see the balance.

We human beings have a certain balance of life or a certain balance of the circles. This balance of the vicious and virtuous circles is the middle way, the balance of the two circles. But more than that, the middle way points the way to breaking away from the circles. If we do not break the circles and do not stop, then we do not come to liberation. We do not have liberated relationships in life.

Life cannot exist without relationships. If we do not have relationship with human beings, we may have a relationship with the Buddha and the Dhamma, his teaching. Some of those who meditate will have a relationship with meditation. We have relationships with one thing or another all the time. Perhaps when we come to the void, emptiness, we will have a relationship with that and to put it more precisely we may say that that relationship is relationship with the whole, of the whole, so that there is no individual being having relationship. Then we will say there is only relationship, the movement of life, the movement of being without becoming. So that movement is similar to what the Buddha said, the stream of Nirvana. That movement is gentle and free in its rhythms because there is no attachment, no ignorance; there is no desire underlying the movement. We should look into this problem of life very close. That is the only way for us to come to liberation in living, without creating crises. Or if we like to create crises we have the freedom to do so, but we must know what we are doing and then there is no psychological suffering. That is putting oneself to the test. You may say that is dangerous, but surely everything is dangerous. Sitting here is dangerous too; we don't know if the building is strong enough; walking crossing the road, sitting in a bus, anything can be dangerous. That is why we need constant awareness of the movement of life, of the problem of life; to be fully aware of all the problems of living in order to see and understand what we are.

Is there anything else apart from understanding and seeing? Understanding has freedom in itself because understanding is not a kind of knowing according to ideas or concepts. When we say 'knowing', we do not mean that we know things according to such-and-such an authority, but we must understand that it means clear seeing, face to face. Then there is no doubt, no perplexity, and that seeing is freedom. At the moment you see reality, the truth, things as they are, you are completely free. You do not need to cry for freedom; you do not need to cry for liberation.

How can we see? We have the eye of wisdom; we can see the truth, things as they are. We can develop the eye of wisdom by looking at ourselves in every moment of living. We may say that if we just look after ourselves we will become selfish; we must do some good things in the world, we must go out and work for the community, for humanity; it is not right just to look after myself, living for myself alone. That is not the meaning of looking after oneself. To look after oneself is to look at everything which is connected and related to oneself. Oneself is not just one unit; one is related to other things, to other people. But one has to look just from this one unit and then expand the looking into all related conditions and elements in life. This looking is not a narrow perception. When each one of us looks after ourselves the world will take care of itself; we do not need to change the world. The world will change if the world of individuals is changed, but without changing individuals there is no hope for change in the world. We try to change the world by building up new ideas, but that is not real change.

So if we would like to have radical change we must look into ourselves, into all the conditions connected with us. In that way we have to criticise ourselves and we have to be in constant revolt against ourselves. You may say you do not like to do that, but life is war and peace at the same time, and by being in revolt against oneself, one knows where one is going. One is wrong, not because of conventions or traditions, not because of religious teachings, but because we do not see clearly. When there is such seeing you don't make war against yourself, but you make peace with yourself. You have more peace when you see where you are wrong and why. Without seeing where you are wrong you can never come to the right. If you try hard to conform to the right action, to the right ideas, you have more and more resistance without seeing where you are wrong.

Life is not so difficult, but it is not easy either. It is wonderful to have life and we have both the negative and positive things in living. We become rich because of going through, but we become very poor if we build a small room to live in, a small room protected by four walls. We may think we are free living in this small room and that the strong walls protect us. But someone else may say that we are living in prison and ask how we think we are free. And they may say 'Break the walls and come out and see how wonderful life is!'

V

KARMA AND MEDITATION

WE DO NOT TALK very much about Karma, the law of action and reaction or the law of cause and effect, in relation to meditation. But I feel it is essential for all of us to look into this law to see how our life is influenced by it. Generally speaking, we talk about the law of Karma in the moral sense; we talk about the law of moral causation, and perhaps to some extent the concept of Karma becomes a kind of dogma for some people. In fact we can see it is not a dogmatic assertion when we say 'This is Karma'. We may say that some person is born with good Karma and another with bad Karma and we see that it has influence in life from the time we were born, and we can see how we become different. We were born from the same family, the same parents, but we are different in our outlook, in our attitudes and tendencies, and in our understanding of life. So what is the reason for people being different, people who may have grown up in a similar environment? They are brought up in the same atmosphere, but are different; the personalities of people are influenced by Karma. If there is nothing particular to an individual, if we are only the product of conditions of society, then we would be the same in all aspects. So if we live in the same society we will all be alike, but we are not only the product of conditions. Yes, to some extent we are conditioned by the conventions of the society in which we live. We have to be very careful today when there is a type of psychology called behaviourist psychology, which denies the inner man, the spiritual side of man. It is said that man is a product of society or conditions, so in order to make man better we have to recondition man. If that is so then we can say that the conditioning process can go on and on without end.

Buddhism teaches a different way. Buddhism teaches the way to de-condition ourselves and that there is a way to end the conditioning process. We say it is possible for any one of us not to be conditioned, to live free from all conditions in society. Coming to this point, perhaps you would like to hear what the

Buddha said about the awakened one. He said the awakened
one grows in the world, but stands above the world, undefiled
by the world. It is like a lotus, born in the water, born in mud
and water, growing in water, but standing above the water,
undefiled by the water. That is the meaning of the possibility
of being free from conditions and from being conditioned. If we
become enlightened, awakened, we will be able to live in the
world without being caught up in world conditions. This is the
way to de-condition ourselves, but we feel it is rather difficult.
Sometimes we may think there is no possibility to live without
any conditions, without being influenced by the outside world
and this is because we ourselves are the conditioned process.
Everything is in us, the conditioning and the conditioned process.

The situations of man, the manifestations of man, come from
the conditioned and the conditioning processes and you ask how
you can live when you are conditioned and conditioning yourself.
How can you get out of the conditions? It is like wanting to
blow out fire by using fire or wanting to clean the saliva off the
floor by using saliva. So it may be difficult for the conditioned
being to be free from conditions. This conditioning process is a
part of Karma. If we do not accumulate anything in life we will
not have any personality, we won't have any attitudes, we won't
have any tendencies, and without these we could be free. But
the fact is that we have accumulated, we have knowledge, we
have experience, we have belief or faith in order to prove that
we exist and can make progress. So what shall we do with this?
The first thing is to understand what we have accumulated and
what we accumulate and why we accumulate. So see into yourself, see all the things you have, whether good or bad; don't be
afraid to see the unpleasant side of life. Normally we want to see
the positive pleasant side of life and we want to cover up anything destructive, unpleasant or undesirable. In that case we
are running away from ourselves. It may be hard to accept
oneself as one is because very often we identify ourselves with
the ideal, with the goal we want to achieve, so that we can
forget ourselves as we really are and that is a very dangerous
thing.

Without understanding this action and reaction in man it is
not possible to come to the understanding of de-conditioning

oneself. The law of Karma, the natural law of action and reaction, has to be considered very carefully and when we understand this we do not need to blame ourselves, to feel that we have done bad things in life or that we have done bad things in the world, that we have created evil in life and in the world. If we come to such action we have to understand why we do so. The understanding of why and how one came to do something which is not right — and we do not speak of right in the conventional sense but in the sense of righteousness or rightness itself — is the beginning of doing the right thing. If we don't understand why we are wrong we can never be right. We may try to conform to the principle, to the precepts, to the rules laid down by wise men, but without seeing why we are wrong, and where, we can never come to the right action. We may try to do the right thing, but when we are in the dark, the darkness of ignorance, trying to do the right thing, it is not possible to do so; it is fooling oneself, deepening one's own conditions and then there is no possibility of getting out of the conditioning process. This Karma refers to both the good and bad aspects of life, the destructive and constructive qualities, action and reaction. Whenever there is action there is reaction — that cannot be avoided. The strength of reaction will be just the same as the strength of action, or sometimes it may be that the strength of reaction will be greater than the action performed in the first place. This happens when the condition and environment of life bring the actor into contact with some powerful or unresolved condition. Then the reaction is very strong. When one understands this one can accept the fact that this is only reaction and one must not try to stop it.

In the history of Buddhism there is the story of the monk called Moggallana who possessed great psychic power, he could even fly through the air and could walk on water. Towards the end of his life he was seized by people who received instructions from his enemies to try to kill him and he was seized in the house by fierce people who surrounded him, trying to kill him. If he could get out through the window he could fly anywhere and he was trying to do this but in the end he realised that all this was happening because of remaining Karma, the remainder of accumulated action, the consequence of which he had to receive. So, realising that, he stopped trying to escape and allowed himself to be killed. The story says that later he gathered together his bones and ashes, became Moggallana again, and then went away and died by himself. So that we can see that even the enlightened person still has to receive the consequences of actions he performed long ago, but Moggallana did not suffer psychologically.

When one accepts the facts of life and understands the situation clearly there is no psychological suffering and one can see suffering as it is. Then there is no illusion. To illustrate this meaning of Karma, action and reaction, I would like to tell you a story. This is a true event, a true incident. It occurred in Thailand not very long ago. There was a monk who held a very high rank in the Sangha. He was a very intelligent, very knowledgeable person and, besides being the first Thai monk to travel to the West, to the United States and Europe, he was also the first to promote Vipassana meditation in Thailand, and because of this he was the target of envy and jealousy amongst other people on the administration of the Sangha. All of these were elders and one of them was also so very intelligent and knowledgeable that the two, like tigers, could not stay in the same cage. He consequently made a plan to destroy the first monk. And he had the opportunity to do this because he was appointed to the rank of Sanghanayaka, which is a leader of monks, like a Prime Minister. When he was appointed to that rank he planned to destroy the monk. This monk, who was my abbot, was accused of having homosexual relations with a novice and of being a Communist. In that period of time Thailand was in a state of confusion and chaos and the Supreme Commander of the Army came to power. My abbot was arrested and put in jail. It is interesting to note that on the day he was arrested, when all the police force surrounded the monastery — a very large one in Bangkok — he was very calm, he did not lose any equilibrium, and he asked the police if he could write a few letters to the people who had to take care of things, which he did very peacefully. I was also suspect in the eyes of the police because I was one of the people close to my abbot, but at the time of the arrest I was working in the library and ignored the situation. It was also interesting to observe that, following the arrest, two policemen who received money from the monk planning to destroy my abbot were killed in a car accident when they were on their way to get more evidence from various sources. Before the arrest a man who was in the Army with the rank of Major-General, who had made friends with my abbot, invited him to go into the country. He showed him different kinds of guns. Then he took photographs which he sent to the police. This Major-General died of a heart attack. The Nayaka of the Sangha, who was later appointed to the rank of Supreme Patriarch, was also killed in a car accident on the way to a ceremony.

My abbot, who we were sure was innocent of the charges made against him, is still alive but no longer has the rank of Chao Khun. He was removed from that rank and from the abbotship and is now only an ordinary monk, although after staying in jail for two or three years he proved himself innocent at the Courts of Law and was released. If this man, to whom so many Thai people owe so much because of his introducing Vipassana meditation, cannot avoid his Karma then we can see that we too have to face it and that may help us to accept our suffering. From this story we can see how consequences come to be, because of evil thoughts, because of trying to destroy someone who is innocent, and it is quite obvious that this happens not only in political circles, but everywhere.

Thus Karma is something we should think about very deeply and know that if we have evil thoughts about someone and try to perform an action out of that motive, then we have to meet the consequences. It may come suddenly or it may come later. Looking at it closely is not creating fear but just looking into the facts. If we understand this, then we have to look into another side of Karma. If we perform an action, believing that this action will lead to such-and-such a result because of moral causation; if we believe that if we do good we will receive good and that if we do evil we will receive evil and act according to that belief, in that case the Buddha said there is no living of the whole life and there is no opportunity for utter destruction of Dukkha. But he said that if you perform an action in order to become experienced it means you experiment with things for the experience of going through, to learn through different aspects of life, and then surely there is living of the whole life, there is the opportunity for utter destruction of Dukkha.

It is interesting to discuss why a person cannot come to complete freedom from Dukkha by conforming to the law of moral causation. We can seen this very easily because that is part of the law of Karma : if we go into circles of Karma by doing good in order to be good, doing a good thing in order to be better, we can never get out of the circles. We want to be somebody, we want to be better, we want to achieve something, but this wanting can never come to an end, can never lead to the cessation of accumulation, the cessation of Karma. Then one lives a very narrow life because one has to conform completely to the idea and one has the tendency to avoid what is true. But we should also understand that if we do commit an evil thing, an evil action, we will meet evil consequences. We may like to go through the experience and see what the evil consequence means. And then we can live all aspects of life and experiment with them. You may say this is dangerous and harmful, but we understand that if a person performs a riskful action with intelligence and wisdom, that person will not go into the trap, will not be caught in the trap of the action. It is like a man who knows the fire is hot, he will not touch it with the full hand, but if the person does not know that it is hot he may grasp it fully and then the hand will be burned. So in learning to understand life in all its aspects, not with the intent of causing harm or danger to other people, but experimenting with things only with the aim of learning, of going through, there is the living of the whole life and we can come to the end of Dukkha. So one should not worry about anything one has done, but at the same time understanding the whole process of action, and the whole structure of it, is essential.

Now meditation is said to be the way leading to the end of action, the end of Karma. How can we come to the end of Karma through meditation ? We meditate in order to be good, to be better, to have more control, to have more insight. If we have such an idea in mind we are accumulating, not meditating. But if we meditate in order to see ourselves as we are, in order to look into all things contained in this body and mind, to see clearly, not expecting a result, not wanting to become enlightened, leaving enlightenment alone, leaving awakening alone, enlightenment

will come if the right action is done. It will come because right
action is done in the sense that one goes through all aspects of
life, one has seen through and worked through oneself. When all
the stuff of Karma has been eaten and cleared away, what is
left? Nothing. Nothing is left and then the darkness disappears;
and then there is light, there is clarity. When there is no darkness
of ignorance one knows, without bothering to say that one
knows. One may point out things but that is not saying 'I know'.

So the attitude in doing meditation is just to allow things to
happen so that one can see them face to face — our fears, our
attachments, our ignorance, our wisdom, our knowledge, our
images. Whatever we have, we let them come to us and we just
look at them. When we just look and see we don't accumulate, we don't try to be somebody, we don't even try to be
enlightened because that is a false idea. Trying to be something
is the process of becoming, and then one can never simply be.
We may be afraid of being nothing. Yes, there is fear — look
at it — the fear of being nothing. Why am I afraid of being
nothing? I want to be something — yes, that is a fact. When
we are afraid of being nothing we have the desire to be something, otherwise we wouldn't be afraid of being nothing. It is
the same thing when we are afraid of doing nothing because
we have the desire to do something. We are afraid of being
lonely, or being criticised by other people — 'Oh, that person is
so lazy, he does not do anything to improve himself' — and
so we are afraid. In society we must be somebody, we must be
recognised, respected, and we try to identify ourselves with a
group; that is the desire for existence, for becoming. Now we
ask if it is possible just to live without wanting to be anything
and yet do the work, live life every day, and if life becomes
difficult, to see why it is difficult, what is wrong with life, what
happens to life. We have a lot of work to do and meditation
can be practised at all times in life. We may have difficulty with
relationships with our friends; so let us look at the difficulty.
Why? Why is it difficult to have relationships? What is wrong
in our mind, what is wrong with our friend? So if we observe
our situation carefully, closely, we learn. Learning never stops.

In Buddhism we begin to learn when we have entered the
path, but if we are just roaming around, walking about here

and there, we don't learn. We may accumulate knowledge and information about Buddhism, about the spiritual life, about religions or any other thing. We can accumulate without end and the world today seems to emphasise the accumulation of information and knowledge. So when we learn we enter the path, and that is the meaning of learning. When we see things as they really are, perhaps we are not completely free from the things we see; we may have attachment; we may have some kind of negative attitude towards the things we see. It does not matter. Just see. See our attitudes, see any tendencies we have. Then we can flow into the rhythm of life non-stop. There is no stopping and there is no tiredness in this flow of life because we have a lot of energy to flow. We are tired at the moment we cannot flow and we have to look and see if we are stuck with ideas. If we have become rigid with something, we cannot flow; we become confused and fight at the moment of confusion and then there is no energy; there are many thoughts and the head is heavy. We see that is because we cannot flow at that moment. So when we flow with awareness, with watchfulness, with observation, then we learn the flowing of life. Life is not something static like a building; it is in a state of flow and flux and we have to understand that. We may think we have to grasp life but we can never grasp it because it is flowing and if we do not see the rhythm of life we get stuck with ideas, attachment to views, attachment to the concept of oneself, the image of oneself, or the image of the things one wants to identify with. So I am outside of life, I don't come into touch with it, and that is difficult. Dukkha arises at the moment we get stuck. If we just flow along with our awareness and watchfulness we don't have suffering. You see the water running in the river; when it gets stuck or something stands in the way, the water has to try to flow on and at that moment the water has some difficulties, dukkha arises to water, but if we listen to it we can understand.

So all kinds of action, all kinds of Karma, whether in the past or recently performed, can come to an end provided one is learning and meditating, or, putting it in our original words, if one trains oneself in meditation then all actions can come to an end. The Buddha used to say that some slight evil action may lead to a very big result for one person, but a small result for another, and that depends on the training. If a person is training himself in the eight-fold path, the Buddhist steps, then the slight evil thing will disappear. The Buddha compares it to a lump of salt put in a glass. The taste will be very salty because the glass only contains a small quantity of water, but if the same amount of salt is put in the sea then the taste will be different. That is what the Buddha means in saying that some slight evil action will lead to a big result for one person but only a small result for another. The aim is to come to the end of Karma. We may think that if we come to the end of Karma we won't do anything, any good things or any bad things. We should not worry about that; when we come to the end of Karma it means that we come to an end of accumulation, we come to an end of action which is motivated, whether by good causes or bad causes. If action is conditioned by a motive it will produce a result, but if action is done for its own sake without having any desire for return, for a result or a reward, then that action is finished within itself. In this way we say we can finish with everything; we act without carrying it over with us, psychologically or mentally.

When insight is clear there is no further accumulation and Karma does not have any influence on us, but if we still have past Karma, past evil things which form our personality, what shall we do? The personality of man can be changed, provided man will change the inward aspect first. If he does not have an inward change of attitude, of structure, of the way of thinking, of the way of doing things, from his heart, from his insight, then there is no possibility of changing his personality. Personality is the product of what is accumulated inside ourselves. The radical change takes place within and then the external changes will follow. So don't be worried about personality, leave it alone, look into oneself and see what is wrong. Don't try to see what is right because that is not important. It is very important to see what is wrong and when we see clearly what is wrong then we begin to put it right. At the moment we see it with clarity we are not deceiving ourselves, but when we try to look for the right thing within us we can easily be deceived and caught up in the illusion, in ignorance, thinking I must remain like this, I enjoy myself this way. Because we want pleasure and happiness we say 'Oh, if I can be like this I will be satisfied. I don't want to be otherwise. I don't want to look at what is wrong in me because I may not be happy, I may be frightened of the unpleasant aspect of myself.' That is the wrong way to look. We may ask how we can know what is wrong. Human conscience can tell us what is wrong without even having the concept of right and wrong. Conscience should have a close connection with the intuition of man. The intuition of man can know what is right and what is wrong but we have to be careful because this conscience may be a kind of internalised belief given to us by religious teaching or by parents or society. If it is the pure conscience it comes at the moment the mind is very silent. In silence there is clarity, there is no doubt at the moment when we are completely clear and at the same time are still and deep.

You remember that the Buddha described a person who understands the truth as like a lake which is clear, with still, deep water. Such a man is wise and free from knowledge and fear. That person can never be attached to anything. The Buddha said in one of the scriptures : 'The mindful exert themselves, to no abode are they attached, like swans who quit their pools, home after home they abandon and go.' Such swans are not attached to a home and go anywhere, since water is everywhere in the world. So mindful people can exert themselves without being attached to where they live, without being attached to their home of old Karma, in the sense of not carrying the old Karma with them. They leave all these things to the past. Yes, the past is operating in the present. It doesn't matter so long as we see it operating now. Look at it. Do not be afraid of it and do not try to put it aside. See how the past is operating by seeing the past as it is. This seeing has the function of piercing into the past and cutting off the influences of the past. Then the past will gradually become powerless and lose its meaning. That is the way we can put an end to past Karma. There is no other way. Not by saying that I must shut myself off, turn myself off, go to the cave or live in the forest. There too my past Karma will operate. If I don't see it I suffer even if I stay in the cave, but if I see it I can stay anywhere, even in a noisy place. If I can look into myself I can learn what is going on and then I will have the ability, the capacity to cope with myself.

First of all I have to accept myself as I am. We may say that there is no self, but there is an impermanent changing self and we have to accept and understand this changing self; to see how it accumulates things in life and creates problems and difficulties. When we see this clearly we have the opportunity to put an end to Karma. What we do is done in the spirit of clear awareness, non-interfering awareness, without hoping for or expecting any result, without wanting to be or to become anything. Then we can do many good things in the world, because compassion and love are there in the heart. There is no end to action, but action done with love and compassion and awareness will not create or accumulate any tendencies. If we can really do things in that way surely the world will be full of peace. Man will understand man, and man will understand nature. Man will understand the world as it is and not as he thinks it is. In the same way, the image we have of ourselves may be different from what we actually are. That is why the thinking process has to be watched. It must not be used for understanding oneself because thinking becomes the barrier to understanding. Thinking is the reaction of the past. Perhaps there may be another form of completely objective thinking which is thinking from the heart. That is not reaction. So we have to learn to meditate in the true sense, not to learn to meditate in order to accumulate experiences, to accumulate insight, but to see things as they are. To see things as they are is the only thing. Nothing more. If we see everything as it is, what else is there? It may be very difficult to see things as they are because we immediately apply our knowledge and information which will lead us to distortion and so we have to be very alert and very careful to use intuitive insight.

VI

THIS MATTER OF SANITY

LET US DISCUSS the matter of sanity in order to see whether meditation can help us to be sane, to achieve sanity in life. It is a problem nowadays, that many people cannot adjust themselves to their situations in life, particularly those who have lost themselves and become mentally unbalanced, those who have been into mental hospitals and when they come back home have found it difficult to readjust themselves to the new situation, to feel at home again. So what can be done about these people, including ourselves?

If meditation is going to be a way of life, it must be able to deal with many aspects of living, otherwise it will become a very narrow limited way. Perhaps we can say that meditation is a way of life and in this way of life there may be many aspects or many things which we do not include, so then we will go to another extreme in life, taking meditation as an escape. I myself do not feel that meditation is a way of living if it is extreme or used as an escape from living, living life every day. So this problem of sanity or insanity should be examined very carefully, but first of all we have to look into ourselves to see whether we are sane or insane. What is the meaning of sanity or insanity? Perhaps we can say that in most cases to be insane is to go to extremes in life. The tendency to go along the extreme ways of living, thinking, acting or feeling is the way of insanity. Sanity is the opposite; it refers to mental health, mental balance and the tendency to avoid every extreme in living, thinking and acting. This is the way of balance.

When we look into ourselves and watch our activities, our way of doing things, we can see that to some extent we are insane, we are crazy and many people are crazy about the spiritual life. So we have to be very careful because to be crazy is to be extreme, so that when we lose balance in seeking and looking for spiritual development in life we can become insane. We can become a problem for ourselves and so instead of searching we are trying to fulfil our desires, our satisfactions,

57

and that is not the real way of searching. It is, rather, seeking in order to achieve, to fulfil the aim, the goal. So if we can stop seeking we will be able to have balance in life. Seeking can lead to any extreme because seeking is based on desire. It is based on the idea of fulfilment and achievement. Otherwise we would not seek. You may ask if we do not seek how can we come across the new thing, how can we find the new way. We can use inner searching. Searching is looking, looking into something by questioning ourselves, questioning our way of living, questioning our culture, our society, but if we are in this state of questioning, looking into what is in front of us, then there is the possibility of finding the new way — not new ideas, but the new way. The new way cannot be defined.

If we are in a state of searching, looking, enquiring, surely we can find that new way of life — and that new way is not a set pattern. We may think that once we have found a new way of life then we must stick to it. But that is making another pattern instead of a new way, and the new becomes old. You may ask, if we take meditation as a way of living, would it not be a limited process, a conditioning process in life? No, because meditation has no pattern, meditation does not create any patterns, any system or formula for us to follow. It is the way of openness, of wakefulness, of alertness. We have to be alert, aware, and watchful all the time and when we are doing that we do not go into a sleep, we are not lost in the world of dreams or the world of fantasy. We can even watch the dreams, the fantasies and memories, but if we have this watchful mind, the meditative mind, we will not be lost in all these things. We become the outsider watching and looking. So there is no pattern to be created by the meditative way of living. Then we can see what it is to become insane because we cannot be completely sane so long as we do not overcome the conditions, the causes and the habits of insanity.

In this connection perhaps we can look into Buddhism, to what it says about insanity. We can take up some aspects or categories described in the Buddhist scriptures concerning insanity in life. The first form of insanity arises out of the desire for self-gratification. Self-gratification includes selfishness. Now if we always look for self-gratification including coming to meditate with the idea that when we meditate we want to have self-gratification, then the aim of meditation is lost. There is no more meditation if we try to satisfy ourselves. In this way people who devote themselves to meditation can become insane. If all the time we look for self-satisfaction, pleasure, joy and all kinds of fleeting happiness, we will fall into this first category of insanity because when we do not get what we want, when we don't get exactly what we look for we create unnecessary suffering and trouble and that will lead us on and on : It is possible to go round and round in the circle of insanity. We speak not only of self-gratification by material success, by material achievement in life or for advancement in status and position in the world, but also self-gratification in regard to spiritual attainment. In following the way of meditation or mysticism, arriving at a very high state of attainment, perhaps coming to the state of infinity of space, infinity of consciousness and the state of nothingness, it is possible to become attached to even this sort of experience and then there is the possibility of insanity. The underlying cause is attachment and we can see that attachment immediately brings about ignorance. If we are not ignorant we will not be attached. When we say love is not attachment people will protest that we cannot love without being attached. People think of love in a very shallow way; they relate love to the physical emotional thing and think that in order to love one must fulfil some kind of physical need or psychological need, but that is not love. Love is not a need; it is more than that. To love is a feeling of being in totality with anything. It has object and it has no object at the same time. When we understand this we will not connect love with attachment. As soon as attachment comes into being, love disappears and then we are left with attachment, we are no longer in love and there is insanity because attachment brings about ignorance : ignorance, not in the sense of lacking information or knowledge, but in the sense of not seeing or understanding the truth. When we ignore the truth we are lost in unreality.

Another category of insanity is hatred and in this are included ill-will, resentment, envy, and jealousy. Envy and jealousy are included in hatred because when we are envious or jealous of somebody or something, it is also true that we are not satisfied with what we have. We feel angry with ourselves. There is dissatisfaction and a kind of sadness. Dissatisfaction comes to be at the moment we are envious or jealous and these two states of mind are included in the category of hatred. We can see, when we have hate or strong resentment against somebody or something, that we can go mad very easily. We are mad or we are senseless because of the strength of the emotion, and when emotion comes to the very highest point wisdom goes to the very lowest one. There is no wisdom when we are emotionally involved with things, particularly when we relate through the emotion of hatred and resentment, and so we have to be aware that we can be mad, senseless or mentally unhealthy in our experience of life. We have to accept, to recognise ourselves as we are, not to try to hide ourselves, saying we are not insane, we are perfectly all right. When we say we are perfectly all right we are trying to deceive ourselves, trying to convince ourselves there is no problem, no unpleasant feeling or emotion. When we feel angry or full of hate or resentment we should look immediately where it is, how it comes to be. The moment we look at this state of mind and know it for what it is we will not fall into the way of insanity. This looking is quite easy to do, but perhaps we forget. The simple way is always overlooked, always forgotten. So if we remember to look, then we will be in a state of meditation all the time in life. It is not very difficult. Perhaps some people may think they are old and their memory is not very good, but we do not need to remember very much. Just remember to look. Also we should be patient in looking. Patience is essential and when we can bear to look we can see deeper and deeper and clearer and clearer. Patience is important so that we do not create any tension. Perhaps we find that the mind, the resentful mind, creates some uneasiness, some restlessness, when we begin to look and then perhaps there is a kind of mental tension. Okay — look at it again! Look at the mental tension. Anything that becomes clear must be taken as the object for looking and then we can prevent ourselves from going mad. We can become sensible.

The third category of insanity is self-deception, which includes confusion, doubt, perplexity and ignorance. Self-deception is the main cause of suffering. It is like a fire without smoke; you can recognise fire easily if you see the smoke but if the fire is burning inside and, because of being covered up by something else, is not giving any smoke, we do not know if there is any fire there and then it is very difficult to avoid falling into the fire of self-deception. How can we know if we are deceiving ourselves? Sometimes in that state of self-deception there is clarity of mind and we think that clarity is a good thing, but clarity itself has to be examined very carefully because clarity can come in this form of self-deception. The mind is clever enough to create anything to satisfy the ego and when the ego is satisfied and well-protected it will say that everything is okay and there is no need to worry. So we have to be very careful about this. How can we know that we are deceiving ourselves? Should we have preconceived ideas that this is self-deception or can we know without words, without the concept of self-deception? If we don't look for a definition, if we don't look for 'how can I know that I am deceiving myself?', then we can know. We have to stop looking for 'how can I know?' and look at what is happening within; what is actually operating in the mind; how the mind reacts to the experiences in life. So we have to watch our reactions and our responses very closely and very deeply, attentively, and then we know, and then there is no question of not knowing. This knowing will not have any context. It does not look for justification or confirmation because it knows without being told, without being coloured by ideas or views. So in this case we have to watch ourselves all the time; what we are, what we are doing, how we do things, what kind of habits we have, what kind of tendencies we carry with us in our way of living and when we look at all these things and watch them whenever they come to us there is the chance of being free from self-deception.

We also have to be careful that we do not have any conclusions in mind, because conclusions can become self-deception. When we come to a conclusion we are fixed with the idea, with philosophy, with knowledge, and then we cannot move. When we are closed we cannot move and then surely we can deceive ourselves. Understanding, intuitive understanding cannot be a conclusion; it is simply understanding which can be put into different words, in different ways, depending on the situation.

Understanding is just understanding, it is not conclusion. We may explain the same thing in different ways to different people on different occasions, so that the looking carefully and being awake in every moment of living can prevent us from deceiving ourselves and becoming confused. The moment we are confused we have to look at the confused mind, how the mind is creating confusion in itself, how the mind brings about conflicting ideas. We see that when we are confused there is no clarity, we cannot take decisions, we cannot move. Don't try to move when there is confusion and don't try to get out of confusion, go into it completely. Go into confusion and look at all the conditions giving rise to this confusion. It is the confused mind, and that confused mind is confusing itself. Then if we look at it, go into it fully, we will have clarity of seeing and the confusion disappears; there is no confusion, there is no doubt, there is no perplexity. Doubt can be either an obstacle or can be used for understanding. If we doubt in the sense of enquiring, questioning in order to see, to understand, then this doubt becomes a factor for understanding, but if we just doubt in order to talk, in order to bring about ideas, or in order to build up a philosophy, in order to show-off or explain ourselves without wanting or wishing to understand, then doubt becomes a hindrance, an obstacle to insight into reality.

The next category of insanity concerns views, opinions and ideas. This particularly refers to attachment to ideas and views. We can see that when we know something we cannot help being attached to our knowledge; we cannot help being proud of knowing and when we are proud of it we are attached to it and build up complicated reasoned structures. We can find the logical way of explaining things, of making things clear, of rationalising, of intellectualising. All ideas and concepts come to be because of attachment to knowledge, to views. So if this kind of thing is perverted and distorted we can become insane. That is why the Buddha rejected all speculative views, all kinds of conjecture, because these things can lead to senselessness and madness. Our heads are full of ideas and concepts; there is no end to them, there is no quietness, there is no silence in thinking. When there is no silence and clarity there is restlessness and attachment so that we cannot be sane, but when we understand how we become insane it is possible to bring about sanity in life. The way of meditation is the way of looking, watching, observing with silence and clarity and alertness and then one can be sane, one can be naturally healthy and balanced. We can see that we can easily drop into any extreme of acting or thinking. So if we are aware of this we will see into everything we do and see if we are excusing and rationalising our actions. Do not have the idea of following a particular way, because if we do that then meditation is no more meditation. Meditation is to help us to be really awake.

If we can wake up fully in every moment of life surely we can be sane, we can be healthy. Any experience in life, whether negative or positive, will not have great influence on us. We will not become distressed or disturbed by any situation or circumstance, and can thus become truly sane. We will not hold on to the idea of reality, like having the idea of this shore or the other shore of life. The Buddha said something about it. He said those who go beyond this shore and the other shore will not be disturbed or distressed in any circumstances, and those people are truly Brahman. That is the word he used, and the meaning of Brahman, as used by the Buddha, is the awakened person, the mentally healthy person, the person without extremes. The phrase 'going beyond this shore and the other shore' refers to those people who do not have any fixed ideas about reality, those who have transcended their preconceptions and can by this become truly sane. That is why they are called the wise, and we say the wise man is the man who is free from bondage and fear. The wise man will not have any attachments, bondage, or fear in life. The wise man does not mean the man of knowledge; the man of knowledge is full of fear because when we know so much and cannot use the knowledge for real happiness there is a state of fear, of uncertainty. So when we want to be sane we have to see how insanity comes about. That is the first thing.

Those who cling to the question, 'how can I become sane?' are wrong. So don't ask that question; see how you become insane. At the moment you know that you are insane you begin to be sane. So in this way you are clearing away all the conditions and causes of insanity. Is it possible for meditation to help people to be completely okay with themselves and the environment, because in our way of living we find it difficult to feel at home with ourselves, with our families, with our friends and with any experience in life? Surely if we are in this constant movement of awareness, if we do not expect anything in return for our relationships, from our actions, from our work, and do things just for their own sake with full attention and without expectancy or hope, then we can feel at home with anything. If we feel uneasy we feel negative, and we must look at it immediately: why this feeling comes, why it arises, instead of saying 'Oh, I feel negative, I cannot help myself; I think I should be positive'. When we do anything we have the pre-conceived idea that 'I should be something' or 'I should have something', and that prevents us from feeling at home, from being harmonious with ourselves. We have the categories in psychological terms, categories in our minds before we do anything, before we look at anything, before we listen to anything; so we are not free.

These preconceived ideas are very dangerous; they bring about concentration. When we have a preconceived idea we keep to it, we concentrate on it, wanting to fulfil it. That is concentration; it is the narrow perception or the narrow way of receiving things, but the way of meditation is attention, not concentration. Attention is the way of openness. First of all we do not have any preconceived ideas, we do not have emotions or conflicts, we just pay attention to what is in front of us, and look. We look fully with the whole heart, with the whole body or with the whole being of ourselves. If you look with the whole being, leaving no room, then you can experience whole or complete clarity of looking and the head disappears. The head disappears because when you look fully you do not perceive anything, the body or the mind, or the head, and when we do not have any context, anything to look with, or anything to look for, we just look completely, and then we do not feel the head. The head, the brain, becomes completely quiet and still and then perhaps when we come back from that looking we may perceive the head again. There is the story of the Zen Master who said that before he became enlightened he saw mountains as mountains, but at the moment he became enlightened, at that very moment, he saw mountains as not mountains, but after that he saw mountains as mountains again. This is not a kind of joke, it makes sense. First of all we know a mountain as a concept, through the concept; we are told it is a mountain — we accept it; we see mountain as mountain. Then, when we become enlightened, fully awakened, we have no idea, we have no concept. The mountain is no longer mountain. It is something or perhaps nothing; it doesn't matter; at that moment we do not care, there is no concern with concept or idea or thought or shape, and then we come back and see mountain as mountain again but in a different way. Mountain as mountain at this time is not the same as mountain as mountain as we understood it before. We can see it with a free mind, with no attachments. So if we perceive beauty in seeing a mountain we just perceive beauty and then finish with it; we don't carry the mountain with us. But before we used to carry the mountain with us, we took a picture of it, put it in the head. Or perhaps nowadays we have a camera and can take a picture to keep somewhere to look at, to remind ourselves of the mountain because we cannot finish with the experience. But after becoming enlightened we can finish with everything, we do not create any more images, keep any more pictures. When we see it again we can see it again, but if we do not see it then that's okay. So we feel at home whether we see it or not.

This is the only way to feel at home. We finish with everything, with every experience. There is no accumulation. That is the end of action and reaction at the same time. But if we cannot finish with whatever we do, with whatever we come to experience, then we are full of pictures, images, concepts, notions and ideas. Too much! The head should be resting. We should have a clear head, the head clear of all concepts and ideas and that clear head will be full of the new, the ever new. And then we can become sane. This is not a burden and is not very difficult, but for those who have been lost, have lost themselves, they have to make an effort to learn to be aware, to learn to look at things, to learn to live with conflict arising between the new experience and the old conditions, because there is always the conflict between these two. So if one learns to live with conflict one can be mentally healthy. We understand that with conflict one can be mentally healthy. We understand that conflict cannot be avoided and we must not try to avoid conflict. At the same time we must not try to create conflict, but just see how conflict arises. There is then the possibility of putting an end to any conflict. The end of conflict comes to be because of new understanding, not because of power; there is no power to remove conflict. Power to suppress conflict is very dangerous. Conflict is a part of life; we are born into life and conflict is there; don't be afraid of it but see it. When we see it we can understand how to cope with the conflict. The problem is that we do not see it and we do not accept it. When we do not see it and do not accept it we become arrogant and this is because we are afraid of meeting conflict. You say 'No, I do not have conflict'. On the superficial level we may feel okay, but deep, deep down we feel disturbed, and to say there is no conflict is not being honest with oneself because there is a deep feeling that something is not right.

So meditation helps us to be honest. First of all to be honest with ourselves; we must mean every word we say; we must not just use the words and not mean what we say; that is surely self-deception. We want to be polite, want to have good manners, to be agreeable, and then we have to say something which we don't mean. That is the way of insanity. So we have to accept ourselves. Perhaps we feel that sometimes it may be essential not to speak the truth, and this is quite simple — do not speak the truth; that is to say, keep silent. In Buddhist terms this is called Right speech. One of the categories of Right speech is that when we feel it is not right to speak the truth we must keep silent. So keeping silent mindfully is the right thing.

VII

THE SEARCH FOR IMMORTALITY

FIRST OF ALL we should see what immortality is, or whether there is such a thing as immortality at all. Why do we search for it, or do we really search for immortality, the deathless? It seems that we are questing, looking for something which we do not really know and yet we may have some concept of what we want to know or want to achieve, like the concept of immortality. If we look into ourselves we will see a kind of discontent, dissatisfaction. When there is no element of discontent we will not move, we will not look for something deeper, something beyond the senses. We have all experienced through the senses but still we are not satisfied with all these sense experiences. There is a state of lacking in man. Perhaps some people would say we are not lacking because we are already complete from the beginning and that we are simply not aware of our completion, our perfection. Yet if we take it for granted that we are perfect and complete, this may be a kind of delusion if we do not really see, if we do not really understand but just believe. The very important thing for life is questioning, enquiring, looking into something which is not clear and which causes doubt because we do not see, do not understand.

We human beings have to develop all aspects of life — emotional, physical, intellectual and spiritual, but we seem to do these things separately and so it is rather difficult not to go to extremes in life, even when we search for the spiritual life. It is very essential to see why we have the tendency to go to extremes and we may say that it is because there is a kind of insanity in us. If man is completely sane he will not go to any extreme either in thought or in action. So sanity means perfect mental health, mental balance, then there is no distortion of thinking and perceiving things. We have to be very careful in our search, that we do not go to extremes; we have to be aware of our tendencies, of all the attitudes we have towards things.

Now the question of immortality: you may say that immortality is something opposite to mortality. In order to understand

67

what immortality is, we must understand what it is not. We have to look into life, go into our experiences and see whether anything within us, anything we experience in life is immortal, deathless. Is there something which is not subject to change and decay? We see that everything, whether mental, physical or spiritual, is subject to change and decay. Whatever is born, whatever is produced or created, is subject to decay and death. Experience in life, experiences in meditation, are subject to decay, and so they too are mortal. And what is the king of mortality? The king of mortality is death. There is a Buddhist term for death, 'maccurāja' : maccu — mortality and rāja — the king. This question of death has to be understood very clearly. If you do not understand the meaning of death then you do not understand the meaning of life. Death is something which is destructive or something which does not produce, does not lead to any positive or creative action. The dead body may be useful in some way; if it is not useful to human beings it may be useful to animals or plants. But what about the dead mind? If the mind is dead, or dull, unclear, full of confusion, of delusion, it is never creative but full of negative things. It is the source of all kinds of disturbances. That mind is always old, it is never young. It is very important to see that the dead mind cannot create, but always produces chaos, disharmony and disturbances, conflicts and contradictions. Do we search for such a mind? No, but we have it. Such a mind really exists in the operation and practice of life, so that we do not have any immortality.

We may also think of the value of life, the values of the world, or the values we create for the progress of society. If we understand, we see that any kind of value is valid only for a certain period of time. It is not always practical, not always applicable to people of all ages and all kinds. The values of life, the values of anything are subject to change and therefore impermanent. We may say we do not search for the impermanent, the dying, but for something which is undying, not decaying, unborn, that which is called immortality. Immortality has so many names but no name really embraces the whole meaning of it. So first of all we must be free from words, from labels. Sometimes when people see everything changing they are frightened, frightened of life, frightened of experiences. They say life is dangerous, life is insecure because there is uncertainty and then there is fear. We have a fear of meeting things, facing things in life, so we are very far away from immortality. You may say if the body is mortal, subject to decay and death so also is the mind, consciousness, feelings, emotions, any states of existence. True. Then what shall we do with them? Can we find immortality within mortality? Can we find deathlessness within death? Surely these states cannot offer, all the aggregates of existence cannot offer the deathless, the immortal, but they can be a vehicle, a boat to carry us to immortality, to the deathless, Nirvana. So we understand how to use the impermanent as an aid or instrument leading us to the goal, the immortality of life. If we do not understand what we have and do not make the best use of what we have, then that which is ours — our body, our mind, our feelings, our states of mind, our conditions of life — all these become burdensome to us. When we understand how to use them they are useful. A person must be wise to make use of the impermanent in order to get to the permanent, the eternal.

How can we use the impermanent as a vehicle to carry us to the other shore of life? We have to have love for the impermanent things, we have to have heart for them, in order not to create any more negative states or negative feelings about what we have. Sometimes we will say 'My mind is so poor it cannot really help me to go further'. There is a use for mind, it can be used if we understand that when the mind is poor it means the mind needs something that is essential for its continuity. It is thirsty, hungry, so we have to give the mind food, but we must understand what its real need is. We have to be fully aware of what is essential and then the mind will no longer be a problem. By doing that you move on because you cannot move without mind, without the body. You will ask whether, when we meditate and come to the state of no-mind, we can move on. When we come to the state of no-mind we can move with creative energy so that the mind does not become a barrier to further movement, and yet that movement does not bring with it the desire for fulfilment. It is only movement within itself, like a movement in the sea. The movement of water in the sea does not lead to anywhere else apart from being in the sea itself.

Then you will ask : having to feed the mind, do we have to follow its commands? We do not need to follow the commands of the mind because, so long as we do not understand what its real need is, the more we give things to the mind the poorer it becomes. So we cannot blame the mind, and it is not right to blame ourselves either. You may think you are not wise enough to take care of the mind. Do not worry about it. The only thing to do is to look at the facts and to accept the facts as they are without being disturbed, without being carried away by any ideas or by any tendencies. In that way we can keep the mind for a useful purpose and develop it at the same time. When the mind is developed it has more strength, more creative energy, more clarity and silence within itself. Such a mind becomes very strong. It will move in the right direction. So there is no problem for this mind.

The developed mind can lead to immortality. Now we ask what is immortality? We cannot give any definition. Perhaps the word we can use here is Nirvana. Nirvana is immortality, the deathless : it sounds so far away but it is not so very far. We may say Nirvana is the end of suffering or, to be precise, we can say Nirvana is the end of happiness and unhappiness. We may say we do not want the happiness to come to an end. It is unfortunate to end some happiness, but so long as we hold on to happiness we are creating or preparing unhappiness or suffering to come. You can see why; the holding on to happiness is the cause of unhappiness. We have to see where we are wrong and see the point where we are holding on, where we are attached. We are possessive of happiness, but happiness cannot be possessed — let it come and let it go. We have freedom to happiness and unhappiness.

Now what is the meaning of the end of happiness and un-happiness? The ending of Dukkha is the Buddhist term. The ending of Dukkha is Nirvana, so Dukkha is really duality : happiness and unhappiness, suffering and joy, pain and pleasure, all kinds of dualistic things belong to Dukkha. As long as we hold on to duality we have to suffer because we still live within the condition of change and impermanence where there is no freedom. The ending of Dukkha is complete freedom, including freedom to be happy and freedom to be unhappy. In this case we can say freedom to be unhappy means you do not care if your body has pain and you understand that you are free to accept it, to accept pain as pain, suffering as suffering. So it stays there and does not go into the psyche, it does not stir up any things within life. Freedom to be unhappy does not mean that a person is trying to create unhappiness or suffering for himself: the wise never do such a thing, but sometimes unhappiness comes because we live in the world and the world is a conditioned state of existence. If we have freedom within us we can look at the unhappy condition of life, at the unpleasant events, and by looking at all these things deeply we are deepening our insight into reality. That is a kind of appreciation of truth and reality. We do not reject pain because the effort to reject brings about more suffering. The only thing is to look and to see any situation in life as it really is. When there is this freedom within, a person has space to move, to live, to be, and that is part of immortality. Freedom can never die because it cannot be produced. Freedom in the real sense is *clear insight* into situations. Whenever we have clear insight into anything in life we are completely free. So operating with clear insight is both the liberating factor and the freedom itself.

If we understand Nirvana as the end of Dukkha, the ending of duality, then we can overcome attachment. We will not be attached either to the positive or the negative. We do not turn away from the unpleasant things in life, but meet anything with our whole strength, with complete attention. When we come to this point we say that we can never die; the body may die, the mind may die, but the being in such a state of freedom and insight is there. We may ask why, if we cannot avoid death, we seek immortality: we all have to die and surely we have to do so before coming to immortality. We have to make it clear that when we say we have to die before coming to immortality this means that the self, the ego, has to die completely, otherwise immortality cannot be realised, for the self can never see immortality apart from the concept or the idea of it. At the moment the self or the ego dies immortality appears, so at that moment there is no see-er. There is no entity that achieves immortality. Here we have difficulty with the language because language has to have the subject, the entity, so when the self, the ego, dies language also dies. Immortality has no language which is produced by sense faculties, by culture, education or tradition, but we can say immortality has a universal language and that universal language has no words, it has only meaning. Since that meaning cannot be put into one word many words have been used to describe immortality, and people feel they understand what it means if there are many terms, particularly positive terms. You know we are deceived by the positive, by wanting the positive things. We are also deceived by the definite. Things must be very definite. When we go to meditate we think the system must be very definite, we think we must have something very clear in order to meditate. If we do not get that we become frustrated or confused and cannot benefit. This is because of grasping the definite. We have to be very careful. Immortality has no words.

Is it possible for any one of us to come to the complete cessation of conceptualisation or verbalisation? We have to try; try to look and to listen, to use the two faculties of eyes and ears without verbalising or conceptualising. See how painful it is, or how unpleasant it is when trying to look at something without verbalising or conceptualising. That pain, that unpleasantness, will awaken wisdom because we have to keep on looking and listening, and then perhaps we can come to the point of the ending of verbalising and conceptualising. We will then know what immortality is and that is why we put it in very negative terms: the cessation of all conditioned things, the cessation of all conditioned states, the ending of everything, is immortality. We are afraid to see because we do not want anything to come to an end. We are very afraid of seeing immortality. We have to see whether we are very honest with ourselves, whether we really are searching for immortality. If we are held back by fear, fear of seeing immortality, fear of the good things coming to an end, then we are not honest in our quest and can never see immortality. Honesty is the very first and last requisite for coming to immortality. You will ask now what are the means, we have to have the means, what are the means leading to immortality? The means are an end. The means cannot be separate from the end but in our thinking we will say the means are one thing and the end another. We look to the end instead of taking care of the means; so we miss the point, the target. Leave the end alone, don't worry about it, or, in other words, leave Nirvana alone. Take care of the means leading to Nirvana and when the means have been realised, you will see that it is the end. Once you come to the completion of the means, then you begin to live, you begin to move into immortality. At the moment we are taking care of the means we are learning. So if we learn constantly, surely we can come to completion of the means.

The Buddha said that *non-negligence* is the means to immortality. It is quite interesting to look into this word 'negligence' because we neglect many good things, essential things, and follow up the unimportant things thinking that they are important to us. The person who never neglects anything has full wakefulness and that person is always wakeful, always alert, aware, observant and watchful; that person does not go into day-dreaming, fantasies or any form of psychological sleep. At the moment we neglect the essential we go into sleep. In particular we can sleep with the means, which we believe lead to immortality or freedom. So we feel very secure, but sleeping with the means is surely the death of life. It is hard to wake such people up. In religious practice we cling to words and dogmatic assertions. Philosophers sleep with their philosophy and never come to immortality. Some psychologists sleep with their methods and never understand what psychology is apart from theory in a book. It is most important to see that in our life and in our search for this immortality we may sleep with the means which we call meditation. We may say 'Oh, I meditate every day — maybe for half an hour, or for one hour — I am very earnest'. If we do that as a routine without being aware of what really happens then we sleep with meditation and in that case some may say that meditation does not lead to immortality. Non-negligence refers to two principles in the Buddhist teaching : the first is *awareness* and the second is clarity of understanding or *clarity of insight*. These two principles go hand in hand. If there is constant awareness then there is clarity of mind. The mind is clear and the mind can be still, so insight can grow. The more we are aware the more insight we have and the more clarity of perceiving, seeing, understanding. These cannot lead us to sleep because real awareness wakes you up. Sometimes awareness is broken and we may slip back, we may go to sleep for a little while, but when we realise awareness is broken we pick it up again. In the process of learning we cannot be perfect until the learning comes to an end. Non-negligence means attending to intuitive wisdom and then immortality will be seen.

We do not say that immortality will be achieved because that would be misleading. It may create in the mind the desire to achieve. The Buddha made it clear that Nirvana is something to be realised not to be achieved or attained. Nirvana is to be seen clearly face to face, with no doubt, no perplexity, no confusion. When we have the wrong idea of entering into Nirvana, of attaining to Nirvana, we create attachment, the tendency to hold on, to possess. We try to possess the thing which cannot be possessed, but that thing can be realised. If we wake up fully in every moment of living, we can see immortality. We ask 'How can we do that?' We learn simply by doing it, by learning to do it all the time, not just to say I learned to do it in the morning or evening. We learn to wake up in every activity of life.

In order to wake up we must realise that we are in sleep. This is a very important point. If we deny that we sleep then we deny reality and that denial will delay enlightenment or realisation of Nirvana. You will ask why we should put an end to suffering or to the duality of life. Things cannot really come to an end. They seem to go on and on all the time, for ages and ages. We are born to this world and things are going on as they had been going on before we were born. Why should we have the idea of coming to an end of things? We have to think about it logically: if things cannot come to an end it is not valid to make the statement that we must come to an end. Suffering may not exist in us but it exists in other people and in other things. Suffering does not really come to an end. Is it possible for any individual to put an end to suffering? It is possible if he knows what the end of suffering means. The ending of suffering is the stopping of the conditions for the arising of suffering. What is the main condition for suffering to arise in life? You will say, desire. Now if we do not have desire how can we live? Desire can keep life flowing. We say desire is energy, some form of energy, so if we transfer the destructive, negative energy of desire to the creative energy for life then desire is no longer desire. So we can live because we have energy for living and we understand the needs of the body and the needs of the mind or the needs of life. When you do not have the destructive energy or desire, you do not create any more suffering. Psychologically we are completely free from any form of pain, suffering or sorrow because we have immediate understanding of the situation. So it is possible for suffering to come to an end, but it does not mean that we have to stop suffering in the world completely. We cannot do that — everyone has to do it for himself. When people put an end to the conditions for the arising of suffering then they will become creative and have peace of mind, and in that way only can the world come to the end of suffering. It is not possible for the whole world to be free from suffering because we cannot force all the people in the world to put an end to the conditions of suffering. It is a task for all individuals.

When we have immortality in life, when we have complete freedom in living and being then others can gain benefit from us. In that way we are spreading the means, or we are spreading the way, to the ending of suffering, because those who come to the end of suffering can have more compassion and love for other people. You may think if you develop your spiritual life and are free from desire, then you will not do anything for the world and you may become selfish because you just want to have peace and happiness. That is not the case. The truly enlightened people, those who have come to an end of suffering, will be loving and creative : creative, not in the material way because there are many who can produce material things, but in the work of pointing out the way, because there are very few who can do this. This then will be their work and that is not selfishness — there are many people searching for the way.

So we will say now that the only way for immortality to come is to have the real quest, to be honest in our searching, in our development of life. Immortality must be seen in this life, not after death, otherwise we are just looking for paradise. The mortal can live within immortality and that mortal being can live with complete freedom and liberation. If we move towards that end we will not have any difficulty or conflict in living.

VIII

ALONENESS AND RELATIONSHIP

THINKING ABOUT THE TOPIC of aloneness and relationship we may feel that they are contradictory, that aloneness is one thing and relationship another, but let us see whether they are the same or different. In this world it seems that quite a lot of us are afraid of being alone, of being left alone. It is quite a great fear in some people but others enjoy it. So we have to look into our problem of not wanting to be alone or the problem of being afraid of being alone. There is a need for relationship, a need for communication, a need for friendship, for companionship. Physically I think we can manage to be alone, but psychologically or mentally it is quite difficult. Perhaps even when you go to the forest and live in a cave you still want a companion or friend to be with you, not in the same cave perhaps, but somewhere nearby. This feeling, or this need, for companionship is quite extraordinary in human beings and before coming to relationship perhaps we should look into this problem of aloneness.

Aloneness may bring about loneliness or it may bring about freedom. Sometimes people are afraid of freedom because they do not understand what it means to be free. When you are free it is said that you are allowed to do things according to your likes and dislikes, and then perhaps you are afraid of doing the wrong thing, making a mistake. That kind of freedom is not freedom in the true sense. So long as you are afraid you are not free. You are afraid to do something, you are afraid something will happen, you are not sure, you are dependent on something, so there is no freedom. Freedom is in action, not in ideas or ideals. So being alone is a very important thing for any one of us. If we have fear we can look into fear when we are alone. If things within us are stirred up we can look at them, we can go into them. When there are friends and things surrounding you, you cannot see all the things within, things are not stirred up, so you may feel all right on the surface. You say 'I am okay', but deep down it is not okay, something disturbing is going on and we do not want to see it, we do not want it to come up, so we turn to something else, to music, to friends or to anything at all. So that is the way to cover up the disturbing influences within us. The people who are afraid of being alone are really afraid of seeing themselves as they are. We are afraid of seeing the unpleasant side of ourselves. So this problem of fear has to be investigated very deeply because so long as we have fear we cannot have freedom. Freedom from fear means true freedom because when we have no fear we feel free to do anything, free to act, free to move, to talk, to listen, to communicate. But if we have fear, even fear of a little thing, it can stop freedom and then there is no insight, no freedom.

One tends to depend on knowledge or experience in order to act and then there is a sort of self-confidence. But this form of self-confidence is a kind of dependence, depending on experience, knowledge and things we have. And yet we can have confidence without relying on the self. If we have self-confidence it means we rely on the self, on the ego, in order to act, to move. But the self, the ego, always acts with the past, it has nothing new to offer. Suppose you watch your mind and let the mind play. You can see nothing new in the mind. It always brings to you things from the past, or sometimes speculation on or projection into the future. So the new cannot be found in the mind, but only beyond it.

It is very essential to be alone. This aloneness plays a very important part in discovering truth or seeing the new in life, in having the new life. This aloneness does not necessarily mean that we have to go away from society, that we must leave our family, or must retire somewhere without seeing any human beings. Perhaps you will live in a cave with a lot of problems coming up: fears, anxieties, worries, uncertainties. You are not alone, because you are with fear, you are with anxiety, and so there is no aloneness. The aloneness we talk about refers to mental aloneness, being alone mentally, psychologically; it means independence. If we are alone when we are with people, talking and listening, if we can be alone without depending on knowledge, ideas, or information, or on the method or technique of understanding something, we can flow, we can flow with listening, we can flow with talking, without being interrupted, because we have aloneness even though we are with other people.

Perhaps we might think of this word alone — alone is : all one. All one means you are alone, you are by yourself and yet you are with everything without discriminating. When you do not have any dependence you open yourself to what is in front of you and then you cannot be swayed this way and that by the opinions of other people. In other words you cannot be cut into pieces very easily. You can be cut into pieces by coming to somebody who says this and going to someone else who says that, and you go with this and you go with that, and you do not know what to do and then you go into confusion and there is no uniqueness, there is no aloneness. So if you are really alone it does not matter. You can listen to anyone, you can talk with anyone, you can listen to any ideas, any opinions or views without being carried away. That requires complete attention and awareness of what is going on, what is happening, what is in front of us. If there is no attention, watchfulness, awareness then there is no aloneness, because we then have to depend on something in order to find out something else. People say we must have the means in order to know, in order to see. But then we are not alone because we rely on the means, thinking about the means : 'how can I come to this?' or 'how can I come to that?'. Aloneness is very essential. Suppose we say we are alone with our own ideas, our philosophy : then we are not really alone! The person who is really alone has no ideas, no philosophy. We wonder how we can explain, how we can talk about things if we do not have a philosophy. Perhaps the talking can go on by itself without conforming to any philosophy, without conforming to any information. Aloneness can bring about wisdom, not knowledge. Knowledge comes about because of dependence, because of accumulation. Being really alone we have no fear that we will have self-pride, that we will be arrogant, that we will not listen to anyone else. The people who are alone can listen to everyone because there is complete open-mindedness. When we are in this state of being, there is no conflict, there is no contradiction, but if we are not alone we have a lot of conflicts, a lot of contradictions, and this is because we rely on words and grasp their meaning. Perhaps the meaning we grasp is different from the real meaning of the words and we do not let go, we want to hold on. Suppose we talk about awareness.

You may have your own meaning of what awareness means, and by holding on to that meaning you do not understand what real awareness is. And then confusion arises. When we are really aware we do not really know who is aware of what, or we sometimes feel we are aware of ourselves being aware, so that there are many things to say.

It is because of the intellectual process working within when one is not alone and one is not completely aware, not completely attentive, that there is room for conflict and contradiction to step in. We say okay, conflict is a fact of life, we cannot really say that we do not have conflict. Or we may say we do not have conflict, but there may be conflict going on. However, that conflict need not bring about conflict to the psychological existence because conflict is only like rain — it is raining. So if it is raining it does not matter, it does not disturb us and we do not have a certain idea about rain, such as thinking that today it should not rain! We let the rain go on its way and we are free, but if we add opinion, or form the view or have the idea about something which is happening, then there can be the kind of conflict that arises because we are not alone. If we can be alone, completely alone psychologically, mentally, we can see how free we are. I can see that some people cannot really listen properly and this is because there is no aloneness in listening. One has certain ideas, certain attitudes, certain tendencies, and when one has problems to think about then there is no flow of listening. So if we put everything aside and enter into the real being of ourselves, finding the right spot to sit and relax, then there is complete freedom flowing with listening, there is aloneness, we leave the body alone. The body does not mind sitting but because the mind thinks about something and the mind cannot be still, cannot be quiet, it creates movements in the body and the body has to do something. Sometimes the mind feels nervous and then there is something to be done about the body. This is because of the lack of aloneness, so there is no freedom and the body cannot relax when we try to do something with it. When we do not let it go, do not leave it alone. The body needs to be alone without the interference of the mind. If we know this we do not try to put the body right or to be concerned with the body too much, but yet we take care, we are aware of the body and the functions of the body. We take care of the body because there is love flowing in that aloneness. Love can get stuck very easily when there is no aloneness and in the case when you are not alone love becomes attachment. It is no longer love but we have the idea that we have love, when in actuality we are attached. This must be understood very clearly and deeply otherwise we identify the false with the true.

So learn to be alone. How can we be alone? First of all we must see why we cannot be alone, to see what is wrong within us. Okay, we cannot be alone, so let us create the situation for ourselves to go somewhere, to sit in the house, in a room, to be alone, to experiment with aloneness, and see what happens. By creating such a situation we can really know what happens when we are left alone, or perhaps we can go to a meditation centre where we will be left alone in the room. We will feel terrible for the first few days because there is a longing for talking, for communicating, for reading or listening to something. That is the real situation in which we can see ourselves. In the summer of 1972 we had a psychology student who came to meditate. For the first two days he was very aggressive because he did not like the idea of being alone. On the second day I came to his room and he asked what is the idea of not talking, not communicating? We eat together in a certain room, at a certain table but do not talk, we have to observe silence. He was quite aggressive to me. I said 'Okay, you can talk about what you feel now. Then you can see that how you react here to silence, to quietness, to being alone is a very good thing, a very good teacher for you : You are a psychology student, so look into it. How is your psychology working?' After that day, after talking, he understood. Now he loves being alone.

I feel sometimes we need someone to point things out to us because we think in a certain way, we think according to our conditions and when we come across something we react. If we react according to the old conditions within us then we will not see what is the meaning of anything new; we cannot understand it because the old conditions are so strong. Then we form our attitudes, and we can have negative attitudes towards the thing we are doing. That is why we must see for ourselves. This is not bad because it is experimentation; and when you see, you can see what is wrong within you. The *seeing* of what is wrong brings about the right action, *not* the trying to get the right concept, the right idea to act correctly. That is perfectionism and it brings about conflict and contradiction in the practice of life. So instead we have to accept the fact, the truth, of ourselves. If we can be alone we can see what is the obstacle to aloneness.

After seeing that, now we can look at the question of relationship. How can relationship be fitted into this aloneness? We can say we can have relationship with the whole, not with the details. In complete aloneness there is relationship with the wholeness. There is no relationship between you and something else in particular, but there is a completely objective relationship, which is the movement of life. There is joy, there is wisdom, there is freedom in that movement of life. Perhaps in other religions they may call it relationship with God, the One Being, the the Supreme Being, but we can say that we have relationship with the wholeness; the words 'you' or 'me' do not exist, the image of individuality does not exist. But in our everyday relationships can we have aloneness and have relationship at the same time? Surely we can and that is the way of life : to be alone and to have relationship. If we are not alone we may have relationship with people, with things, but that relationship is based on desire, attachment. We want something in return from that relationship. We want to use the people we have relationship with for our pleasure and happiness, and we do not care whether people will be annoyed by our relationship so long as we can get happiness or pleasure. So that kind of relationship is not relationship in the real sense. It is taking advantage, looking for benefits. We can also have a relationship with meditation, for example. When we meditate we are related to meditation and we ask how we can manage our relationship with meditation. Do we want something from meditation? We say that we want peace, stillness, silence, insight from meditation. But the result of that desire for a return is that meditation will go away. If we can be completely alone we will see that we are very aware, very attentive, because we cannot rely on anything. And we can then understand that at the moment we feel we can rely on something, we go to sleep. 'No, no', we say, 'it doesn't matter, we feel secure now, we don't want to do anything', so we sleep with our method, we sleep with the means we have when we ought to be using it. But when we are left alone we become very intelligent, we have a lot of wisdom arising. Even if we have pain or suffering that pain and suffering can awaken wisdom in that moment of being alone. The Buddha was left alone just before he attained to enlightenment; he was completely alone under that tree on the bank of the river. When he was alone he was tempted by Māra, the evil one, which means that things within him came up which he fought. Later on he realised that it was wrong to fight and so stopped fighting and then Māra disappeared. Then the Buddha came to enlightenment. One can look into things very deeply when one is alone.

Hopelessness is something very helpful. When you feel you are hopeless it means you have no hope for life and that is the very beginning of the new wonderful life you will have. So we must not take the unfortunate situations in life as something destructive but as something to be used for waking up or for looking into the depths of life, and then we can have relationship with anything we have. We can have relationship with ideas, with thoughts, with experiences and we understand that relationship must be based on understanding, freedom and love. When we can manage our relationship with ourselves first of all, then it is easy to manage relationships with other people. Suppose a husband and wife have a poor relationship. Who creates the disharmony and conflict in that relationship? Do not blame husband or wife. Both of them should look into what is wrong in the relationship. By looking into what is wrong with ourselves we can be alone and then we can have our relationship in the light of this aloneness and can see what is wrong between us. As soon as there is such wisdom, things can be put right, so that husband and wife can have a good relationship. They have to understand that they do not depend on each other in order to be happy, to be secure, to be safe, but yet they can contribute constructively if they are aware of their relationship and if each one is alone in their relationship with life, with each other.

The Buddha said that good companionship is the whole of the holy life. When the relationship is right, harmonious and based on understanding, freedom and love, then the holy life is lived in the present moment, in every moment of life. We cannot

be without relationships and deep relationships come with aloneness. Aloneness allows real relationship. At the superficial level
there is relationship between one person and another, between one
thing and another thing. If we can look into superficial relationships from our aloneness and see how we relate ourselves to our
friends, families, relatives, nation, country or culture, and look
into relatedness in life, seeing how conflict arises in relationship,
then we are building real relationship. We do not wait until
we see everything clearly in order to have good relationship
because this will grow from the moment we go into what is
wrong and what it means to have relationship. Then life is
flowing, life is moving deeper and deeper into reality.

You may ask if we can have relationship with people who are
difficult, who are restless, unconcentrated and not interested
in spiritual development as we are. Can we have relationship
with them? Surely those people need relationship and yet you
are afraid you may be misled, you may be turned away from
your spiritual quest, you may be completely conditioned by those
people, and so you avoid them. In that case you do not have
aloneness, and real relationship cannot come to be. In real
relationship there is no discrimination whether a person is right
or wrong, one can learn from all people when one has relationship with them. Learning can really come to be at the moment
of being alone in relationship. This is important. If you cannot
be alone you can never learn. If you stop relationship you can
never understand all aspects of life. But perhaps you will say it
is difficult to understand all aspects of life because we cannot
live long enough; we may live for sixty, eighty or a hundred
years at most. If we can be alone in our relationships, in every
moment of life, then we learn and we know. Perhaps we won't
be able to explain what we know. It does not matter, do not
try very hard to explain, otherwise the learning will run away
again. At the moment we want to explain, then we are not alone.
We try to conceptualise and there are so many words in our
heads and the head is no longer clear. The mind is not clear.
The mind is full of words, pictures, conversation, talking, so
there is no quietness. Let the mind have peace because it has
been working the whole day. Sometimes in sleep it has to work
with dreams, so we should have compassion for the mind. Let

it be alone. When the mind is alone it is very intelligent, it has a lot of creative energy for life. There is no contradiction at all between aloneness and relationship.

We might think it is very hard to have this objective relationship, the relationship with the wholeness, without having images, without having anything in oneself. This is only an idea, only an opinion. Suppose we let ourselves flow. We flow with people, we flow with things, and surely when we flow we have awareness and can let ourselves flow without having any idea to obstruct, and then perhaps gradually or suddenly the image of oneself will be put aside. We are there but there is no 'me' who is there. When we are listening with complete attention, then the perception of the head and body completely disappears, but we are not frightened of that because there is complete relationship with what is going on. Still the feeling of being there is recognised, but it is only a feeling, there is no image, no picture, and that is quite close to the relationship to the whole. When we go on doing that in our life then we can manage relationship with people very well; there is no self-consciousness. Self-consciousness really prevents relationship and it prevents people from being open, being natural, being spontaneous: because of tradition here in this country, or in this house, we must conform to something and so the flow is stopped. If you can flow with awareness and see whether awareness can take care of your relationship, then you can understand how to manage your relationship, how to be free. It is not something so high or difficult to do. The difficulty lies in the thinking, conditioned mind, and when we cannot experiment because of fear or uncertainty then it becomes more and more difficult to have objective relationship.

If we can manage to have this objective relationship we can be in harmony with anyone. If we do not have the concept of race then we will not discriminate. People may come from different parts of the world, they may have different nationalities, but that is something for social convenience only, not something real, and when we are together there is no American, no English, no Thai. We are just human beings. Yes, somebody might come from Thailand, someone else from America or any other place, but those are only places. The mind is free from nationality and race. Somebody may have a different colour of skin but that does not matter because when one is born in a certain place then the colour will be different. So there is no discrimination. We can have relationship with any one when we are alone. So this form of relationship can open the way to world nationality, world citizenship. But there must not be the idea of some kind of organisation. It must come from understanding, not from organisation because when it becomes an organisation it becomes limited and is something separate from other organisations, and then there will be strife between one organisation and the other. This is a universal relationship we can manage and then we can love; love and compassion will flow naturally in our relationships. Then we can recognise individuality, because there are certain differences according to training, education and culture, but these differences should not be taken as obstacles to the universal relationship, and perhaps we can learn different things from different people without accumulating knowledge : learn by knowing, recognising, acknowledging the other things apart from what we were taught.

Then what is the problem? If people understand this and live life according to this we can have peace and harmony in the world. There is communion of life everywhere, there is no identification, separation. If everyone can maintain aloneness inwardly the mind is very free to work, the mind is free to work with insight into the situations in life. That is the real need for everyone and perhaps if this method can go to everyone in the world then surely we can have world peace. But first of all we have to start with ourselves, put ourselves in the right way and then we can be a mirror and go everywhere. Everywhere we go we have the mirror without anyone carrying the mirror, and then other people can see and something new may come to be in the world.

IX

BASIC MEDITATION

Now WE SHALL go into some other aspects of a system of meditation, Vipassana meditation, without too many complications or complexities. This is the true Buddhist meditation, and it is a very simple meditation. But the simplicity is always overlooked so that we do not see the profundity. We look for the profound, but when we overlook the simplicity we pass it and do not understand the truth and profundity of things.

What is the whole spirit of Vipassana meditation? The whole spirit of it lies in full attention or complete attention. This is very important. If we actually attend to what we do, what we see, what we come across, what we experience, then there is no waste of energy, no waste of time for seeing the truth, the living movement of life. In the Satipatthāna Sutta you can see that the Buddha advises us to attend to all the things we do in our life; whether we are walking, eating, lying down, standing, talking, looking forward, looking backward or keeping silent. All this must be done with full attention so that you do not miss the point, the target, of meditation practice and you do not live in the past or in the future, but fully in the present. The Buddhist teaching emphasises the full living in the present. Fully living in the present is the whole point of Buddhism.

So this full attention is the means leading to the capacity or ability to live fully in the present and, in fact, the means is the end in itself. So you must not look to the end, but to fulfil the means and then the end is not separate from the means. Now in life we should examine ourselves, to see whether we are attending to everything fully, and to find out what is the obstacle to attending to everything fully if we cannot do this. It may be because we have thoughts, fantasies, so many things going on in the mind, that we are not really there; the body is there but the mind is somewhere else, wandering around seeking something, or entertaining some thoughts. So the mind is not attending to what is actually going on at that moment, and then there is no attention.

To start with, attention may be a little bit narrow because you want to focus your attention on some particular thing so that you can get to stability or steadiness within. But in that attention, for example, if you are focusing your attention on the talking, on what is being said, you let yourself flow with listening and the mind may become concentrated with what is happening in this room. There is a point in the mind, but this point is a moving point in which there is no distraction, or interruption, if the mind is actually attending to what is being said without expecting, wondering or thinking. Later, when you come to full attention, the mind is opening itself, becoming expansive in its consciousness to see the whole, without grasping concepts or ideas. In that wholeness of seeing or listening you can sense some stillness or serenity, joy or tranquillity. So attention is very important.

One other thing we should understand is that when we pay attention to something we tend to be serious in the sense of being tense, being stiff somewhere in the mind or in the body. When there is no relaxation of the body or the mind, attention is a kind of mental creation, not the natural process of paying attention. The natural process of paying attention is to let things flow, not to obstruct, not to exclude yourself or anything else. Then the whole process of attention is an inclusive process, which is the dynamic process of living, the dynamic process of life. Some people may call this a kind of movement in silence, or movement in the unknown. The unknown is that which cannot be given a name, a concept, but we already have a concept in Buddhism, even for the unknown. We do not need to look for the concept. What we need is to come into it and see it face to face so that there will be no doubt or uncertainty. To meditate in your daily life is to be very attentive to everything. Even to be attentive to the inattentive is very important, and may be something to which you have never been attentive before. Then you can feel lively with your life, with your experiences, without being attached. That is a point I will return to later.

So to meditate is to be aware, constantly aware of your experiences, your life. In this awareness, in this constant awareness, you can see that there is aloneness, there is clarity. Tiredness of the body, or heaviness of mental states, can be cleared away if there is constant awareness. The body may feel tired if it has been used for some time but when the mind is kept free there is no interference from the mind and then the body can adjust itself so that relaxation and tranquillity or calmness will come to be. It is not very difficult to be attentive providing we are not conforming to the idea of being attentive. This is an important point. If you always hold in your mind 'I must be attentive', that is wrong. Don't say 'I must be attentive'; I must be attentive without having the idea of being attentive.' Just attend to it! As now you are attending to the talk — just attend to it. Then everything becomes very simple. The difficulty arises because of our ideas, or preconceived knowledge, preconceived notions. That is why knowledge is one of the ten corruptions in Vipassana meditation.

Why does knowledge become an obstacle to meditation, to the flow of intuitive wisdom? Because knowledge belongs to the past. It is a kind of memory, conceptual thought; it is accumulation. So the past exists in memory, in experience. When we try to apply knowledge to the new challenge we are only reacting according to the conditions we have, so that we never go beyond our conditions. We are Buddhists so we react to the situation according to Buddhist tradition, Buddhist belief. But belief is a limited experience and we will not be able to cope with the whole situation. If we are free from our Buddhist traditions and beliefs, and the knowledge we gain from Buddhism, we will be able to open ourselves, put ourselves into the new challenge fully and see what happens. The true Buddhist knowledge is always there because the Buddhist knowledge exists not only in the scriptures. Wisdom is found in the scriptures, but often people misinterpret the wisdom in the scriptures and then they hold only the ideas. They get interpretations, explanations and then there must be something wrong. But if one actually comes into contact with wisdom one can be free and then one can meet any challenge freshly and completely. The whole thing is attention.

Soon you will walk away, you will go back home; you may go by car or by train or by bus. If you attend to your going you don't see only yourself, you attend to everything going on in that process. To be attentive does not mean that you have to keep to the one point without looking aside, because if you do look to the whole point you can see what is beside the point, and also what is underneath the point. So if you attend to the full thing in the point, the point becomes a very wide subject, a wide field, so that you cannot miss anything in it, which is very important. Travelling by train you may say 'I must be attentive so I will close my eyes and enjoy my meditation, looking into myself, without looking out to see the beautiful trees or fields or anything else'. What is the difference between experiencing joy by closing the eyes and looking into yourself, and looking out of the windows seeing the landscape and the things outside with full attention, without thought, without any imagination? There is no difference. Joy is the same whether you can see inside yourself or outside yourself. It is joy. So in attention there is no thought, there is no imagination, there is no projection. Conceptual thinking is completely abandoned, so that we can have objective understanding.

Objectivity. I am looking at you, listening to the talk. If I am looking at you with thoughts, or with some ideas, I see you according to what I think, but I don't see you as you really are and there is no objectivity. Or you are looking at me with a certain condition in your mind; you see me as a certain person, and somebody else will see me as a different person, so that I am two or three persons in myself. This is not objectivity in seeing. Yet if we are objective we can see reality. We may put it in different words, in different terms. The whole point is to be attentive all the time. You never get sleepy, you never get dull or drowsy if you are attentive, and you never get tense. There is no tension in attentiveness. Tension comes because of hope, expectation or fear. You can become tense very easily, especially when there is great fear of something. Then your body starts trembling. You notice when people have fear that the body shakes and this is very often seen in meditators, and also when people have pain. When pain is very strong there is shaking of the body, trembling and crying. Some people cry — some very loudly. Why is that? It is because of fear, the fear that I may be hurt or destroyed; something wrong may happen to my body or to my mind. Fear comes together with pain. Thinking of pain can strengthen fear and fear can bring about some physical phenomena. That is very obvious. With full attention, if you have pain, you give full attention to the pain to see how pain comes to be, how it develops and how it passes away from moment to moment, and then you can see fear. The mind may try to create fear, and then you can catch fear, or the tendency of the mind to create fear. Everything is noted and then pain will be seen objectively as it is and fear will not come to interfere.

Then you will be able to maintain equilibrium, steadiness, stability, stillness of the body and stillness of the mind. This is very important, but when we have pain we have the idea that we must do something, change our posture. This is because we look for comfort. In Buddhist terms we can say the change prevents us from seeking Dukkha, pain, sorrow, suffering; and the continuity of things, the endless continuity of things prevents us from seeing impermanence. You don't see impermanence because things continue to be, and because things are put together and have a unity we don't see the reality of things, but see only a unit and take it as an entity, a self, a substance. But when you look into that unity you see different things put together. You cannot find an entity, a substance. It is a combination. So that is why we have to look into the details. Attention will help us, first of all to see the whole, or the appearance, and then to see the details. If attention is continuous or going on steadily there is a faculty of looking into the details of what is going on. Without seeing the details there is no true Buddhist analysis. The Buddhist analysis is really looking into the details. When we see the details we understand immediately this is this, this is that. Through the understanding of the parts one can come to the seeing of the whole; the wholeness will be seen. Or one can come into the whole and then see the details. We can go either way. Attention is the *only* means because in attention there is awareness and in awareness there is attention. In practice, attention, awareness, and watchfulness cannot be separate. They work together hand in hand. The first thing is to pay attention to something, and in that attention we do not look for something, we just look at what is actually happening, going on. When everything is there, meditation can be practised in every movement of life — whether you read, talk, wash the dishes, cook, drive a car, do anything — meditation is there. Proper meditation is to live fully in the present, or to realise that the real life is living in the present, not in the past or in the future.

In meditation we pay attention, we are aware, watchful, observant. What is the prime aim of doing this? What is the goal of meditation? A Zen master said there is no goal because meditation is the goal itself. The goal of meditation is meditation, as the goal of life is living. So don't look for the goal. In the Satipatthāna Sutta we can see that the Buddha said that awareness or mindfulness is established just for pure insight and awareness. Only that! We meditate, we cultivate awareness, mindfulness, just for understanding, for awareness itself. Nothing more. But in that understanding, that awareness, you reach the right path; you overcome sorrow, misery, pain and you realise Nirvana. When awareness becomes complete, total, the aim of it is awareness and understanding; you understand. Now in this case when we understand and we are fully aware, there is no clinging or attachment to any world; the world of the body, the world of feelings, the world of the mind or the world of mental objects. Cling to nothing common in the world. What does this mean? Do not belong to the world of the body, do not cling to the world of feelings, do not cling to the world of the mind and mental states, or anything at all.

Basic meditation does not really have any fixed object, but we have something to start with. We have a preliminary object, the Touching Sensation : When you breathe in and out, you do not interfere with the breathing process, you just let the breath come in and go out as naturally and as normally as possible. You perceive, you feel, but you do not visualise. I want to emphasise that you do not visualise your body, but feel the movements going on in the body according to and responding to in-breathing and out-breathing. These movements are called the Touching Sensation. When you feel, it will be in your diaphragm, in the whole area of your abdomen. The area does not really matter, but, rather, the feeling of the movements. The sensations which enter your consciousness should be observed, should be the focus for attentive awareness. It may be like holding a mirror. You are looking in the mirror of the movements, the sensation, the Touching Sensation, without naming, without saying, but only observing, watching non-verbally, in order to see how the movements come and go. But when you are attentively aware, you will be able to see the physical process working, including the calming down of the physical activities and releasing of some tensions or sometimes observing that the body is not flowing properly: We sit in a certain way. It is not your habitual way. You may have some stiffness. You may have some pain or discomfort and then what should you do? We don't say that you ignore discomfort or pain, but you attend to pain, you attend to discomfort in order to see clearly first instead of moving the body and then you will understand how discomfort develops and how you become tense, or how the body becomes tense. You observe it as a process, clearly, and as you are doing that, you are developing your patience. And when you have patience, you can look more.

If there is any reaction, you can attend to your reaction, so that the whole thing is observed. If you just look at your reaction, you do not judge the situation. There is seeing and observing without judging, but with total awareness to see the observer clearly. It is like holding a mirror. You look and you can see yourself watching yourself. It may be that you have such an image in the beginning, but gradually this image of an observer will die away from your consciousness and then you become more and more objective in your observing, and awareness becomes more objective, which gives you more freedom to work. When we do this, we attend to whatever happens: after watching these movements in the body, whatever is distinct and evident is taken as the object for meditation.

Sometimes we have an interesting thought, or some disturbing thought, or a memory of something unpleasant in your life. Then we have to pay full attention to that, to see how this comes back. Look at it! See, allow it to go on, don't be afraid, don't avoid. By doing that you go through anything coming into your consciousness. You go through and work through so that things will be cleared up. You will say your inner house will be clean and clear, you will feel lighter and clearer and more at home with yourself.

In sitting it is essential to keep the back straight, particularly the position of the head, the back, and the spine. These three parts should be in an upright and balanced position. The benefit from this posture is clarity of the body. When we sit like this for some time, we feel really balanced, even though the legs may go to sleep occasionally and we do not feel clear, or we may have some tenseness : Later on, the head becomes clear and light. The body also becomes light. So that is the benefit of the right way of sitting, and it gives a benefit to our body, and the body can become more flexible and healthy. Therefore in sitting : keep the body erect and the mind alert. Rather, attentive awareness should be always present. Instead of holding on to an object, you hold on to the principle of *attentively alive awareness.* When it is broken, pick it up. When it is broken again, pick it up again. Instead of trying to grasp the object, apply the principle to make it stronger and more stable.

In regard to awareness of feelings, when we pay attention to feelings, whether pleasant or unpleasant, or neither pleasant nor unpleasant, whether that feeling is worldly or spiritual, we just see it, observe it as it is. When you see the feeling without the feeler, you understand feeling as it is. Thinking about the feeling — Oh! the feeling is so painful, or very pleasant, or exciting, it's marvellous today — that is the world of the feeler. At the moment the feeler says something there is no actual feeling, but only thinking. This is a very important point. Suppose you have a particular feeling, very distinct to you at that moment. That feeling must be the object of your meditation. So now I have the object, that is, the feeling, so I must go into the details of the feeling. The feeling is not a thing in itself. It is a process. You must not see only the appearance, the development of feeling, you must be able to see what is the condition, what is the originating factor of this feeling and see whether this feeling belongs to worldly experiences or if it belongs to spiritual matter, something beyond you. We have to see all this, otherwise we don't see the feeling. When we understand the arising, the disappearing of the feeling, and the interconnection between the feeling and its associations or factors, we see the whole process of feeling and then there is no one who feels, but feeling

exists. The Buddha said only feeling exists, there is no feeler
behind it. We must come to that point, otherwise there is no
meditation.

Whatever you take as the object of meditation you have to go
into the full details of it. By going into the details of anything,
I must warn you again that you must not apply your knowledge.
Knowledge is corruption, the corruption of insight and its main
obstacle. Don't carry anything when you attend fully. Let your
wisdom take care of itself. We have wisdom, we have power,
and we must let it work. Do not suppress it. In the Christian
sense it is said 'Let God act through you'. In Buddhism we say
let our intuitive wisdom act on us. At first we may find it
difficult because we are heavily conditioned by our knowledge.
We feel insecure if we do not think, I must do this and I must
be a very thoughtful person. What is a thoughtful person? The
person who thinks about method, and about experiences, and
that delays and postpones. But when you attend spontaneously
you are very thoughtful without thinking. The truly thoughtful
person has no interfering thoughts because he attends to everything with his heart. So we call him the thoughtful person. He is
wise, intelligent. Do not be afraid of getting into insecurity, or
uncertainty, or harm or danger if you do not think. Unnecessary
thinking can waste your energy; a lot of energy is expended
wrongly because of that thinking. So if you store your energy
you can work, you can live creatively, peacefully, happily,
because the whole point is just to understand, just to know,
through awareness. What is the aim of knowing? The aim of
knowing is just knowing!

Coming to another aspect of Satipatthāna (the practice of
mindfulness), we see that the Buddha said, in regard to the
mind, that we must understand the mind in any state, the mind
with lust, the mind with hatred, the mind with stupidity,
ignorance. When the mind has a slack state then it becomes
a little bit drowsy, what you might call pleasantly drowsy — like
taking a trip — then it is the slackened state of mind and you
just know it. When the mind becomes expansive or when the
mind has a mental state which is superior to itself, you just know
it; the mind is being with that state. When the mind is liberated,
understand it, know it as it is. When the mind is unliberated,

know it as it is. This is a matter of knowing, only. It is our fault when we want to control, want to be free, want to avoid. When the mind becomes slackened we say 'Oh, it is terrible now, I must do something with the mind; it is slack and I must not allow it to be like that'. So the 'I' steps in, wanting to get rid of slackness, the slackened state of mind. When there is distraction you get frustrated because you want to be undisturbed, undistracted. This is our fault and we must see it as a fault. The Buddha said clearly in the Satipatthāna Sutta 'Know such a mind as it is, look at it, attend to it, and then see what happens'.

Normally when you attend to the slackened state of mind it gradually becomes clear and then the slackened state disappears. There is clarity coming instead. If you attend to it you can see. Do not attend to it with any idea, the idea of avoiding it, removing it, overcoming it, or with the idea of attending to something. Do not have the idea, do not carry ideas, and then you are very free to look at the mind and its state. We have many things to do with the mind if we try to make an effort, but our doing is only reaction. So we never do anything with it. Can we ever do anything with the mind? We only react to it, according to our conditions, our desires, our hopes. We must be simple, look at the mind, and see it as it is. Then we can come to stillness, serenity, silence and understanding, with clarity, through attention, full attention. So full attention is with everything. Do not be too lazy to find out. When you are lazy you think you must wait and ask someone who knows. That is postponement — a kind of laziness. But because it has been a habit for a long time we do not know that we are lazy. The beginning of understanding this can help us to go further — if we know how to deal with the mind.

Many beginners say 'When I start meditating my mind is everywhere'. Do you really know that the mind is everywhere, or do you just think it is? You do not attend to it. If the mind is everywhere, let it be, let it go. Your duty is only to look at the movements of the mind, attend to every movement, every activity, see how far the mind can go. You must be an outsider, the witness, in the way of looking at the mind. But when you are an outsider, you have something to do too and that is not to have the image of looking at the mind. We always create an image. We do not exist in reality, we exist in image. I am such and such a person with certain aspects and my self is looking at something now, attending to something. So you let the image occupy your self, and then there is no attention because you are occupied by image. There is only reaction. But when I say you are an outsider, I mean that you do not get involved emotionally or mentally. When you do not get involved, you actually attend to every movement of the mind and you see whether the mind can stop moving. At the moment the mind stops moving, what is emptiness, what is clarity, stillness? What does it look like when you come into actual stillness? Is the stillness something created by you? So we have to see it very clearly, by giving full attention to it. There is nothing to do, in fact, in meditation, but there are many things to see . . . until we come to seeing nothing in particular.

By this, I mean that when we come to the transformation of concepts we actually see reality. Concepts are like clouds, covering the truth. Words may be useful if we know how to go to reality through the words, but for the majority of people the words are a great obstacle, because words are taken as truth. Like the Buddhist term 'Dhamma.' We do not really understand what Dhamma is. We say 'Oh, Dhamma is the teaching of the Buddha, Dhamma is the truth.' What is the teaching of the Buddha? You may explain it in many words. And what is the truth? Words can be either useful or dangerous to the understanding of truth. We say we cannot communicate without words. But can we communicate with words only? We can communicate without words sometimes. In fact, when the disciple and master understand something together there is real communication in that moment, and in that moment both the disciple and master become completely silent—at the moment of understanding the truth. In fact, each one of us must be both disciple and master. A disciple is someone who is learning; the master is someone who is giving instruction. You can give instruction to yourself and then you can learn. The learning process is going on and on. This is a kind of self mastery. If one is fully aware, totally attentive, in every moment of life there is no waste of time.

THE MIDDLE PATH OF LIFE